Child Protection
and Parents with a
Learning Disability

of related interest

Parental Learning Disability and Children's Needs
Family Experiences and Effective Practice
Hedy Cleaver and Don Nicholson
ISBN 978 1 84310 632 6
eISBN 978 1 84642 744 2

A Practitioners' Tool for Child Protection and the Assessment of Parents
Jeff Fowler
ISBN 978 1 84310 050 8
eISBN 978 1 84642 209 6

Mastering Whole Family Assessment in Social Work
Balancing the Needs of Children, Adults and Their Families
Fiona Mainstone
ISBN 978 1 84905 240 5
eISBN 978 0 85700 484 0

Risk in Child Protection
Assessment Challenges and Frameworks for Practice
Martin C. Calder with Julie Archer
ISBN 978 1 84905 479 9
eISBN 978 0 85700 858 9

The Child's World
The Comprehensive Guide to Assessing Children in Need
Second Edition
Edited by Jan Horwath
ISBN 978 1 84310 568 8
eISBN 978 0 85700 183 2

Child Protection and Parents with a Learning Disability

Good Practice for Assessing and Working with Adults

Including Autism Spectrum Disorders and Borderline Learning Disability

Penny Morgan

Jessica Kingsley *Publishers*
London and Philadelphia

First published in 2017
by Jessica Kingsley Publishers
73 Collier Street
London N1 9BE, UK
and
400 Market Street, Suite 400
Philadelphia, PA 19106, USA

www.jkp.com

Library of Congress Cataloging in Publication Data
Names: Morgan, Penny (Clinical psychologist), author.
Title: Child protection and parents with learning disability : good practice
    for assessing and working with adults--including autism spectrum disorders
    to borderline learning disability / Penny Morgan.
Description: London ; Philadelphia : Jessica Kingsley Publishers, 2017. |
    Includes bibliographical references and index.
Identifiers: LCCN 2016008981 | ISBN 9781849056793 (alk. paper)
Subjects: LCSH: Family social work--Great Britain. | Learning
    disabled--Family relationships--Great Britain. | Parents with mental
    disabilities--Services for--Great Britain. | Children of parents with
    disabilities--Services for--Great Britain. | Child welfare--Great Britain.
Classification: LCC HV700.G7 M67 2017 | DDC 362.30941--dc23 LC record available at
https://lccn.loc.gov/2016008981

British Library Cataloguing in Publication Data
A CIP catalogue record for this book is available from the British Library

ISBN 978 1 84905 679 3
eISBN 978 1 78450 186 0

Printed and bound in Great Britain

This book is dedicated to the girls –
Holly, Jess, Ellie, Cerys and Robyn.
With thanks to Paul, Rose and Corrina
for their help and advice.

Contents

Chapter 1

Introduction

As we move further into the twenty-first century, the response of society towards people with a learning disability continues with its slow process of change from protective, parental and disabling towards enabling and life-enhancing attitudes. This shift in attitudes underpins the change in lifestyle from institutional care to fostering independent life in the community, which, in turn, is accompanied by a consistent increase in the numbers of people with a learning disability becoming parents. We also know that parents with a learning disability are over-represented in child protection investigations, more likely to be subject to a care application and more likely to lose their children than any other group of parents (Booth, Booth and McConnell, 2005b). However, as Cleaver and Nicholson (2007) point out, social workers assessing these parents will not be specialists in learning disability and may not even have access to specialist training, advice or support in working with what are often families with a complex agenda of needs. The purpose of this book is to unravel some of the threads which make up that complex agenda of need and to provide social workers in the field with a strong frame of reference to enhance their everyday practice.

Models of care

Societal responses to people with learning disabilities usually echo the dominant theoretical perspective of their time. They tend to reflect three frames of reference – legal, medical and social – with the balance between these perspectives varying according to the current context. Examples of people with intellectual disability have been recorded since biblical times. In the Middle Ages, the emphasis was on a legal differentiation between 'idiots' and 'lunatics' linked with early ideas about capacity – the former being innate whilst the latter was regarded as temporary. This approach continued into the fifteenth and sixteenth centuries, with courts using criteria such as numeracy and social skills to determine competence. A Florentine intellectual published the *Archipathologia* in 1614 which takes these ideas further, distinguishing between intellectual disability, mental illness, dementia, and delirium, recognizing that these conditions originated in the brain.

Distinguishing between so-called madness and what we now term as learning disability continued as a theme, being confined to mental illness. More formal testing of people began to be developed toward the end of the nineteenth century, triggered by universal school education, and continued throughout the twentieth century. Categorization was introduced, with terminology reflecting perceived ability.

The medical model became increasingly used to define disability during the twentieth century. It relied on understanding a person's problems or behaviour in terms of illness, diagnosis or treatment, giving professionals the role of qualified experts, and restricting the agency of the person with a learning disability to one who needs control and protection. Hospitals were built (often Victorian workhouses or parts of asylums were re-purposed) for the 'inmates' or 'patients', with a basic treatment ethos, which was more likely to equate to containment.

During the latter part of the twentieth century, the social model of disability began to be regarded as a more appropriate way of providing services. In this model, the impact that society has on restricting people that are not the majority is considered, focussing on the person rather than the disability. This model underpinned the Government White Papers, *Valuing People* (DH, 2001) and additional follow-up augmentation and review papers (DH, 2007, 2009, 2010c). These set out service principles of rights, independence, choice and inclusion. This model has been the background to the major change in the provision of services from institution to community during the latter part of the twentieth century and into the twenty-first. If this began a trend towards increasing the numbers of parents with a learning disability, then it was supported by the Human Rights Act 1998 which includes the 'right to a family life'. It has been observed that increases in the number of parents with learning disabilities have been reported in all countries which have moved towards all services based on 'ordinary life' principles and community living (King's Fund Centre, 1989).

Terminology

Confusion surrounds the classification of and terminology used when discussing learning disability. A range of terms exist which vary in offensiveness, correctness and fashion. Outdated terms such as *mental subnormality* and *mental handicap* are rarely used; terms such as *mental impairment* and *severe mental impairment* were used in the 1983 Mental Health Act but this was revised in 2007 and now uses the term *learning disability*. *Mental retardation* was still, until relatively recently, the 'official' term used in North America, but now *intellectual disability* and *developmental disability* are the preferred terms.

The term *intellectual disability* is starting to appear in much of the United Kingdom and international literature and is currently the preferred term used by the International Association for Scientific Studies of Intellectual Disability and in the *Journal of Intellectual Disability Research*. Currently in the United Kingdom, the terms *learning disabilities* or *learning disability* are commonly used within the National Health Service and in Department of Health documents.

Some self-advocacy groups prefer the term *learning difficulty* as they consider this to be a less pejorative descriptor. The problem here is that this is not consistent with any of the 'official' terms described earlier and can be confused with the term *specific learning disability* – a term primarily used in education to describe a processing disorder which affects the ability to understand or use language, the most common of which is dyslexia. The processing difficulties are likely to result in particular problems with reading, writing, spelling and mathematics – not the generalized difficulties we see in learning disabilities. Specific learning difficulties are independent of cognitive abilities, but there is an apparent gap between the student's ability and actual achievement.

Definitions

Although this terminology is relatively new, definition of the underlying condition has remained largely as it was prior to any semantic changes.

Two major systems are used worldwide in the classification of mental health disorders, which includes learning disabilities. They are the *Diagnostic and Statistical Manual of Mental Health Disorders* (DSM) developed by the American Psychiatric Association (APA, 2013), and the *International Statistical Classification of Diseases and Related Health Problems* (Chapter 5) from the World Health Organization (WHO).

The DSM is essentially a national (US) diagnostic classification of mental disorders, widely adopted by US government agencies and worldwide, particularly in Western Europe. The newly published DSM-5 (replacing DSM-IV) uses the term *intellectual disability*, with *intellectual developmental disorder* as an equivalent term (ID/IDD). Intellectual developmental disorders (IDDs) are defined as those 'with onset during the developmental period that includes both intellectual and adaptive functioning deficits in conceptual, social and practical domains' (APA, 2013, p.33).

The WHO publishes the *International Statistical Classification of Diseases and Related Health Problems* (current publication ICD-10, WHO, 1996). A working group for ICD-11 proposes replacing *mental retardation*, used in ICD-10, with *intellectual developmental disorders* (IDDs), which, it is hoped, will achieve some consistency with DSM-5.

The ICD-10 (WHO, 1996) defines mental retardation as: 'A condition of arrested or incomplete development of the mind which is especially characterised by impairment of skills manifested during the developmental period' (WHO,

1996, p.259). The proposed ICD-11 (which will supersede this definition) is likely to describe IDDs as characterized by a deficit in cognitive functioning prior to the acquisition of skills through learning.

The British Psychological Society's (2000, p.3) guidance on the assessment of learning disability cut through these labelling inconsistencies and emphasized the key components of assessment or diagnosis as 'a significant impairment or intellectual functioning; a significant impairment of adaptive behaviour (social functioning); with both impairments arising before adulthood'. These three key components are seen in both the DSM-5 and ICD-10 (and proposed ICD-11) diagnostic criteria and will now be explored further.

Diagnostic criteria

The three key areas which need to be assessed for a diagnosis are:

1. intellectual functioning

2. adaptive behaviour and social functioning

3. age of onset.

Intellectual functioning

Intellectual functioning, also called intelligence or cognitive ability, refers to general mental capacity, such as learning, reasoning, problem solving, planning, abstract thinking, judgement and practical understanding.

Intellectual functioning is usually measured with an intellectual quotient (IQ) test. There are a variety of individually administered IQ tests in use in the English-speaking world. The most commonly used individual IQ test series is the Wechsler Adult Intelligence Scale (WAIS) and the Wechsler Intelligence Scale for Children (WISC) for school-age test-takers, although other tests may be used. Generally, an IQ test score of around 70 or as high as 75 indicates a limitation in intellectual functioning.

IQ scores have what is called a normal distribution – that is, most people score around the middle, or average, range with a few at either pole. Many human attributes are distributed in this way – for example, height: most people are average, with a few very tall or small exceptions.

Figure 1.1 shows that we would expect about 2.2% of the population to score below 70 – that is, in the learning disabled range – and a further 13.6% in the borderline range – that is, between the average and learning disabled ranges. So, quite a small number of people are likely to have an IQ below 70, but, because of the high demand that being a parent places on the individual's skills and thinking, the additional 13% in the borderline range may also have specific difficulties associated with their cognitive profile: a much higher number of people.

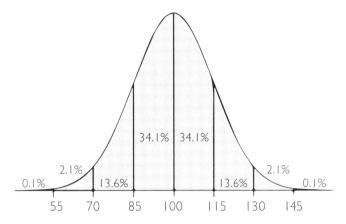

Figure 1.1 Normalized IQ distribution with mean 100

Add to that the proposal of some researchers that the borderline range is artificially enlarged by social deprivation (people not reaching their full cognitive potential because of socio-economic factors and so skewing the evenness of the normal distribution), and we have an even larger population of parents with very specific needs to consider.

Adaptive behaviour

Adaptive behaviour is the collection of conceptual, social and practical skills that are learned and used by people in their everyday lives.

Conceptual skills include language and literacy; practical concepts such as money, time, number; and self-direction. These skills are important in the organization of everyday life, and are frameworks with which we manage competing demands and choices.

Social skills include interpersonal skills, social responsibility, self-esteem, gullibility, social sophistication and social problem solving. These skills help us to navigate the social demands of living in a community with others. They help us to understand the basic rules of society and follow these rules or laws; they also help us avoid being victimized.

Practical skills refer to the activities of daily living such as personal care (washing, dressing appropriately, personal grooming) and household routines (cleaning and cooking) together with wider, community-based skills such as occupational skills, healthcare, travel and transportation, safety, use of money and use of the telephone.

Standardized tests are available to define adaptive behaviour profiles and provide peer comparisons, although real-life observation and interview is a reliable source of information.

Age of onset

This condition is considered as a developmental disability; that is, there is evidence of the disability during the developmental period, usually thought of as occurring before the age of 18. This differentiates learning disability from conditions that have been acquired later in life through some kind of trauma (such as an illness like meningitis or a road traffic accident resulting in brain injury) and which will have subtly different presentations.

Additional considerations

All sources which seek to define and describe learning disability emphasize the importance of a holistic view of the individual where the community environment typical of the individual's peers and culture is taken into account. Linguistic diversity and cultural differences will affect the way people communicate, move and behave, and should be included routinely as part of any assessment.

Prevalence

The Government White Paper *Valuing People* (DH, 2001) recognized the difficulty in producing precise information about the number of people with learning disabilities due to problems with diagnosis and definitions.

Statistics suggest 2.2% of the population will have an IQ below 70 with mild learning disability more common than severe or profound learning disability. Historically, there has been a general consensus that the overall prevalence of moderate and severe learning disability is approximately 2–4 persons per 1000 of the general population (LDO, RCGP and RCPsych, 2012), although recent progress in medical treatments has led to predictions of an increase of 1% in the next 15 years. These figures are due to increased life expectancy, survival into adulthood of children with complex disorders, a rise in the reported numbers of people diagnosed with autism spectrum disorder (ASD) and greater prevalence amongst some minority ethnic populations.

A systematic review of 43 prevalence studies suggests that the incidence of mild to moderate learning disability is more likely to be 3% of the population (Emerson, 2003). Social deprivation is cited as a contributing factor in increased incidence over statistical expectation. Later meta-analyses conducted on worldwide populations suggest higher incidence rates of up to 10%, but these are subject to cultural variation and disparities in definition.

Estimating the numbers of parents with a learning disability is a similarly inexact science. Historical data is minimal; given early beliefs that being a parent and having a learning disability was both incompatible and undesirable, little attention was paid to the issue. A few studies in the US have collected data from which they have extrapolated figures – some 36,500 parents as a very conservative estimate in the US; Holburn, Perkins and Vietze (2001) cite a figure of seven million parents with learning disabilities reported in the 1993 US census: again, considered by the authors to be a low estimate. In the UK, Emerson *et al.* (2005) reported that, from a survey of 2898 adults with a learning disability, 1 in 15 was a parent, but the selective nature of the data makes these figures rather uncertain. In the UK, there is general agreement amongst those working in the field that the numbers of parents with a learning disability seeking support from services has increased significantly since the mid-2000s.

An additional group which is not usually considered in these discussions is people who fall into the *borderline learning disabled* range of scores. That is, they cannot be diagnosed with a learning disability, but cognitive impairments are evident and these impairments may, to a greater or lesser extent, affect everyday functioning. Although it is clear that some parents with cognitive abilities in this range will cope with the task of being a parent, some, who have low levels of parenting knowledge and experience and who are subject to significant stressors, are likely to struggle. As they are an indeterminate group, the range of services and supports on offer are likely to be more limited than those offered to a parent with a diagnosed learning disability, and mainstream support services may overestimate a parent's ability to participate. As this group constitutes a minimum of 8% of the population (with estimates being higher when social deprivation effects are factored in), the potential for the need of an informed supportive service is evident.

Aetiology

The causes of intellectual disability are diffuse, and the efforts to identify causality are not always successful. In general, the greater the severity of delay, the more likely the origin or cause will be uncovered. History, physical examination, imaging studies, chromosomal or genetic evaluations and metabolic testing all contribute to the identification process, but clear causality cannot always be detected.

The causes of learning disability may be best categorized as those with onset before birth (prenatal), during birth (perinatal), or with postnatal onset. However, severe psychosocial deprivation – less easily quantified – is also cited as a contributory factor.

Prenatal causes

These are factors – both internal and external – occurring during pregnancy that affect the development of the foetus and particularly the development of the brain.

ABNORMAL BRAIN DEVELOPMENT (CEREBRAL DYSGENESIS)

During foetal brain development, billions of cells of varying types continuously form and move to distinct locations; skull development also progresses. Any event that interrupts this developmental process, such as lack of brain growth or abnormal development, can result in malformed or missing areas of the brain. This in turn may lead to a loss of brain function, the significance of which will vary with the location and area involved. Malformations of greater severity lead to one or a combination of conditions such as epilepsy, cerebral palsy, specific and generalized intellectual impairment, and sensory impairment.

CHROMOSOMAL OR GENETIC

In this group of causes, genetic malformations – which may be inherited from either parent or may be a spontaneous occurrence – affect the future development of the newborn child. Some may be identified at birth, others as the child grows. Some syndromes are unlikely to be seen in parents. For example, Turner's syndrome affects only females and is associated with infertility, and Angelman's syndrome is generally associated with more severe levels of learning disability. However, the two commonest genetic syndromes may occasionally form part of a patent's diagnostic profile.

Down's syndrome is the best-known and most common chromosomal disorder associated with learning disabilities, occurring in 1 out of every 800 births. An error in cell division during prenatal growth results in an extra third chromosome 21, called Trisomy 21. Everyone born with Down's syndrome will have some degree of learning disability and share a number of similar physical characteristics – for example, low muscle tone and specific facial features – although there is considerable variation from person to person. A proportion of people with Down's syndrome will suffer from medical complications (e.g. congenital heart disorders, digestive and bowel problems) which vary in severity.

Fragile X syndrome is the second leading genetic cause of learning disabilities and the leading genetic cause in males. It involves a genetic anomaly of a gene located on the X (sex-determining) chromosome, which is why it is described as 'X linked'. Behavioural features include hyperactivity, tremors, stereotyped movements, poor coordination and a reluctance to make eye contact. Social and communication skills are not well developed; people with this syndrome may have historical diagnoses of both learning disabilities and autism.

PRENATAL INFECTION

Acquired maternal infection during pregnancy can result in developmental delays in the child, which are later diagnosed as learning disability. The rubella virus was a common example of this kind of infection, with damage occurring as the rubella virus passed across the placenta and attacked the developing nervous tissue in the unborn foetus. In recent years, the prevalence of congenital rubella has declined with the introduction of rigorous immunization programmes.

Prior to this, maternally acquired syphilis was a common cause of learning disabilities, but due to the availability of effective treatments is now much less common.

Some severe viral infections may cause complications in pregnancy, potentially giving rise to encephalitis (inflammation of the brain), with a subsequent effect on the cognitive development of the foetus.

TOXIC EXPOSURE

The potential for adverse foetal effects in response to maternal exposure to drugs and toxins is well established. Alcohol, nicotine, cocaine and heroin have all been associated with increased risk to the foetus, including the risk of developmental disabilities. Some prescription-based medications may also present a risk to the developing foetus and should be regularly reviewed by the mother's general practitioner (GP).

Exposure to environmental toxins also raises the risk of later development of learning disability – for example, exposure to lead, mercury and radiation.

Perinatal causes

At the perinatal stage, during delivery, restriction of the oxygen supply to the foetus can result in brain damage. Complications in delivery, such as the use of forceps or suction, or the umbilical cord becoming wrapped around the baby's neck, contribute to a raised level of risk to the developing brain.

Infants who are extremely premature – born at or before 25 weeks of gestation – have, if they survive, the greatest risk for long-term effects. There is a high incidence of long-term neurodevelopmental impairment and chronic health problems in these children, the effects of which are diffuse and lasting.

Postnatal causes

Once the child is born, environmental factors have a significant part to play in brain development.

NUTRITION

Severe malnutrition and significant deficiencies of a range of vitamins and minerals will impact negatively on the developing brain.

INFECTION

Maternal acquired infection may affect the foetus prenatally, but, once born, a number of acquired infections may affect the child directly. Examples of conditions associated with later diagnosis of a learning disability include:

- herpes simplex virus

- streptococcus

- human immunodeficiency virus (HIV)

- meningitis

- encephalitis.

TRAUMATIC BRAIN INJURY

Insult or injury to the brain, whether accidental or non-accidental in origin, will have a significant effect at this stage because of the vulnerability of the newborn infant and the interruption of the continuing intense developmental process.

TOXIC EXPOSURES

Exposure to drugs and environmental toxins, as in maternal exposure during the perinatal period, is associated with raised risk of the development of learning disability to the newborn infant and young child.

SOCIAL-EMOTIONAL FACTORS

Children who are deprived of attention and stimulation, whose basic emotional needs are not met or who are actively violated may not reach their full potential either in terms of cognitive or social development. Studies examining samples of children from Romanian orphanages report that children growing up in institutions providing little or no emotional or social interaction and stimulation have measurably different brain structure from other children, affecting both specific skill development and connection between areas of the brain.

Multiple causes

A person's learning disability may not be attributable to one single factor or area, but may be caused (or is likely to have been caused) by a combination of factors before, during and after birth.

National strategy

Having considered the 'basics' of diagnosis, prevalence and causality, we will now look at the national picture for the provision of services for people with a learning disability.

The government produced the 'Valuing People' group of white papers beginning with *Valuing People* (DH, 2001) and continuing with a number of additions and reviews: *Valuing People Now: From Progress to Transformation* (DH, 2007) and *Valuing People Now: Summary Report March 2009 – September*

2010 (DH, 2009). These papers represented the first national strategy statements in this area for 30 years. They outlined future government strategy and vision for people with learning disabilities as one which ensures that people with a learning disability have the right to lead their lives like any others, with the same opportunities and responsibilities, and to be treated with the same dignity and respect. Four basic principles underpinned this vision:

1. rights – having the same human rights as anyone else

2. independent living – having greater choice and control over the elements of daily living: housing, education, employment, leisure and participation in family and community life

3. control – having appropriate information and support so that informed decisions about people's own lives can be made

4. inclusion – being able to participate in all the aspects of community.

The necessity to offer support to parents with a learning disability was recognized, but in no more than general terms and with no specific recommendations about how this should be delivered. The matter of what parents with a learning disability might expect in terms of service provision has therefore largely been left to 'best practice'.

What is good practice?

Good practice guidelines have been published by the Department of Health and Department for Education (2007); the Scottish Government produced *Supported Parenting: Refreshed Scottish Good Practice for Supporting Parents with a Learning Disability* (Scottish Consortium for Learning Disabilities, 2015). This is based on the DFE guidance, but updated somewhat, and contains a useful 'resources' appendix.

Both these papers agree that good practice demonstrates five key features, some of which relate to the overall planning of service delivery and some to the delivery of the service itself. These are:

1. accessible information and communication

2. clear and coordinated referral and assessment procedures and processes, eligibility criteria and care pathways

3. support designed to meet the needs of parents and children based on assessments of their needs and strengths

4. long-term support where necessary

5. access to independent advocacy.

However, whilst it may be tempting to read these guidelines and feel that certain recommendations are the province of senior management, each of these recommendations, to a greater or lesser extent, may be translated into everyday face-to-face work with clients. We will now look at these recommendations in more detail and consider how they might be woven into casework.

Accessible information and communication

This recommendation emphasizes the importance of good communication as part of helping families to engage with services and limiting the sense of frustration and lack of control often engendered by the assessment process. Providing accessible, easy-to-understand information in a range of formats (large print, pictorial, via DVD, face-to-face) and offering this information at the appropriate time is part of good communication. Finding ways of helping people to understand and remember what has been decided at a complex meeting (e.g. a child protection meeting) is another part of the communication task. So, whilst it could be argued that the system as a whole should have a policy of providing choices of information formats, and procedures ensuring that meetings are parent-friendly, there is much that the individual can do to promote communication. Establishing a parent's preferred communication method is important – for example, texting to make or remind about appointments is often helpful, but not for the parent who keeps his phone switched off to avoid contact with an ex-partner. Communication involving reading and/or writing can be difficult as it involves admission of difficulties, which may be hard to do, or painful reminders of failure at school, and these issues must be handled sensitively. Simply taking time to consider what you need to communicate and how it might be done is helpful. You also need to allow sufficient time for matters to be explained and discussed, and make sure that others involved in the parent's life (e.g. schools) use the same accessible approach. If you can be client-centred and creative, then any subsequent work will be more effective. In *Supported Parenting* (Scottish Consortium for Learning Disabilities, 2015, p.17), the People First (Scotland) Parents' Group list key messages about communication:

Explain things clearly so you really understand.

Don't use jargon.

Make sure you understand reports.

Listen.

Take time to communicate with us.

Turn up on time.

Ask us what we need and want.

Give us a choice.

Tell us about independent advocacy.

Follow things up – on time.

Are honest if they can't do something.

Treat us as individuals.

Give us information in the format that we need on time.

Clear and coordinated referral and assessment procedures and processes, eligibility criteria and care pathways

This recommendation covers both clear pathways within a service and between services (joint protocols), in particular protocols between children and families' services and adult learning disability services. Some services achieve this via protocols covering all parents with additional support needs; some are more specific. Others include health, education and housing. Whatever the arrangements, such joint protocols will assist you in enabling families to access the range of services they require, so it is a good idea to become familiar with the provisions of any local arrangements. If there are no local agreements, the Social Care Institute for Excellence has published an excellent resource for the development of joint protocols and, where a joint agreement has been reached, many Social Services' websites will have this available to the public. As a practitioner, you are in a good position to represent to managers the benefits of working to joint protocols.

It is perhaps easier for the individual practitioner to consider the local pathway – good working relationships between teams based on personal knowledge are invaluable. Fostering good communication between different agencies can be achieved via protocols, but identifying and making personal links with key individuals, say in housing, education and the local Community Learning Disability and Community Mental Health, Maternity and Health Visiting teams, is invaluable. Often communication is impaired because we simply don't understand the way other teams' systems work; a quick telephone call to a friendly administrator may ease the way in this instance.

Dawn's story

Dawn is managing to care for her two-year-old really well. Her social worker has said she is pleased with Dawn's progress and sees that Dawn is using ideas from the 'toddler time' group she attends. Dawn has short periods where she feels really down and that she can't cope – these are interfering with her progress. Antidepressants from her GP have helped a little, but not much. Dawn is assessed by the Community Mental Health Team who say that she doesn't have any serious problems and is not eligible for a service from them. The Learning Disability Team say that Dawn is coping well with her flat and daily life, so she is not eligible for a service from them either. Dawn's social worker goes online to check whether there is a joint local protocol in place. There is, so she emails both team managers and her line manager pointing this out, requesting a further meeting. In the end, the learning disability service offers Dawn an assessment and, after this, eight sessions with a community nurse to discuss past issues they think might be related to her low mood, and anxiety management. This helps Dawn to learn how to cope with her low moods more effectively.

Support designed to meet the needs of parents and children based on assessments of their needs and strengths

This might seem self-evident, but it does highlight the tendency to adopt a one-size-fits-all approach. If we wish to put support in place for parents, then this must be based on a good assessment of needs and circumstances and addressed by the parent's own view. Parents with learning disabilities are entitled to use universal services – these services are required under the Disability Discrimination Act to make 'reasonable adjustments' for their services to be accessible. However, this recommendation encompasses the hidden issue of whether, how and why we identify parents with a learning disability. Mainstream services need to be prepared to identify and support parents with learning disabilities (Llewellyn *et al.*, 1998), but how do they *know* who needs additional support? It could be argued that some parents have no wish to be singled out as different, but James (2004) points out that women with learning disabilities report poor experience of antenatal care. We have to work towards providing a range of supports aimed at meeting the range of need which presents in the community from accessible information to joint working between Community Learning Disability Teams and midwifery.

Long-term support where necessary

This is a wide-ranging requirement which many practitioners would agree they find frustrating. It is self-evident that the family that struggles to care for a young child is likely to struggle at other points of the family life cycle. As one parent said: 'You don't find out on your twenty-first birthday that your disability has gone away – it's there for life.' It is unfeasible for local services to provide a dedicated service, so it makes best sense to equip services ordinarily involved with the skills to support families, at least in the first instance. Local health visitors and nursery staff can be a source of support for the parent struggling with the changing behaviour of the pre-schooler, with schools being the main focus for older children. It does help to have one lead support professional who can take on a signposting role, guiding parents through the maze of statutory services to get the help they require. The voluntary sector has a good record for providing support in specific areas, but again it's a question of finding out what is available in your area and being able to involve parents. Walking into a roomful of strangers is intimidating for most of us and particularly difficult where parents may lack confidence. A 'buddying' system, for example, could help overcome this particular issue.

Access to independent advocacy

We all hope that at times in our lives when we need extra support someone will be on hand to speak up for us, or we will be able to make our own voice heard. People with learning disabilities are at risk of being ignored for a variety of reasons; they rarely hold positions of power, may find the communication element a challenge or do not have the social skills to be assertive, to name but a few. Parents need to be heard when they are talking about the difficulties they are having, when they are trying to explain what support is needed and especially when the balance of power is with the statutory organization rather than the family. Advocacy is about speaking up, working to promote choice and making things happen and change; it is not about acting as a referee, taking control or replacing professional roles. There is no right kind of advocacy; it can be offered in a number of ways:

- *Case advocacy* focusses on one issue, or a set of issues, and is likely to be short-term. The support may be needed because the work to be done requires specific expertise (e.g. education, housing or law), or there is a temporary increase in decisions to be made or changes to be accomplished.

- *Self-advocacy* is the most effective form of advocacy when people are willing and able to speak for themselves. Many people with learning disabilities can speak for themselves if only people will give time and space to listen. Being aware that self-advocacy must be encouraged and promoted and that in order to do this you need to allow extra time and build confidence is an important first step.

- *Peer advocacy* is when the advocate and partner share similar experiences such as having a learning disability or mental health problem. It works on the principle that people who have experienced the same circumstances have more insight and can offer effective support.

- *Paid independent advocacy* is invaluable where volunteer advocates are not available. Generally, independent advocates are unpaid, but volunteers are always in high demand and short supply. Some represent the interests of people with a learning disability to provide an advocacy service, usually offering a combination of independent and citizen advocacy. Statutory services may contract with an independent organization whose provision will be localized in order to identify possible contacts, explore local groups or local branches of national organizations who promote the rights of people with learning disabilities, or people with disabilities in general.

- *Citizen advocacy* is a partnership between two people – the advocacy partner and the citizen advocate. An advocacy scheme usually matches up the advocate and partner. The matched citizen advocate volunteers to speak up for and support an advocacy partner whose wishes and choices are being actively sidelined or ignored. He is unpaid and seeks to identify, but not influence, the partner's wishes and decisions in a trust-based relationship. The partnership is seen as long-term and consistent but can be dissolved by agreement of both parties.

A survey of 14 parents' views of the support offered by specialist (paid independent) advocacy services through the child protection process (Mencap, 2007) found:

- The parents believed that they were treated with more respect by professionals when their advocate was present.

- The parents felt they had better understanding and more of a voice in the process.

- The emotional support offered by advocates was a seen as a significant contribution.

- The advocates, who had some knowledge of child protection, were able to challenge professionals' practice on occasion.

The research concludes that whilst these advocates were not able to change the overall situation, they helped to prevent bad practice and disempowerment whilst reassuring professionals that the parents were appropriately included in the often complex child protection process. To date there are no national practice recommendations clarifying the role of an independent advocate in such proceedings, which is long overdue.

Maria's story

Maria, aged 21, attended special school and completed a Skills for Life course at college. She lives in her own flat in sheltered accommodation and looks after herself well. Maria recently had a short-term relationship with a man she met online. Now she is pregnant and has been unable to contact this man, who seems to have disappeared. Maria's mother and father are very upset by her pregnancy. Maria's mother, worried about the family history of mental health and learning disabilities, wants her to have a termination. Maria has decided to continue with the pregnancy, but is very scared and feels alone and unsupported. She has been to several planning meetings at the local children's centre. Once, Maria's friend went with her, but her friend told her that all the people at the meeting wanted to take her baby away from her, so Maria didn't find this helped. Even though everyone at the meetings tries to explain things to her, Maria is so worried her sleep and appetite are starting to be affected. The thought of possible future care proceedings terrifies Maria.

Maria's social worker introduces her to Jane from the local advocacy service, a charitable organization part-funded by a service agreement with the County Council. Jane is able to attend meetings with Maria. Jane explains simply what is being said at the meeting to Maria, encourages Maria to speak up and helps Maria write down key words so that she remembers what has happened. Although meetings are still difficult, Maria is learning to cope with them much better, with Jane's help. Maria knows that if she has to go to court, Jane will go with her to help her stay calm and understand what is being said. Maria does not feel quite as helpless as she did and is growing in confidence.

Accessing services and support

In summary, although it is often frustrating working within a system which does not automatically prioritize the needs of parents with a learning disability in line with government rhetoric, there are many steps we are all able to take to make individual practice more effective and enabling. Find out whether your area has a joint protocol; if not, suggest developing your own. If you have a protocol, keep a copy on your desk and use it to access services and support.

Take personal responsibility to develop a learning disability-friendly approach in the language you use and the support materials you access. Make links with your local learning disabilities teams – face-to-face contacts are always more effective than letters or emails. Consider the role of advocates and whether you, the person himself or a friend, relative or family member can act as an advocate. These are initial steps and ideas; the next chapter goes on to consider more fully how to engage and work with parents who have a learning disability.

Chapter 2

Mild Learning Disability and How it Affects Parenting

In this chapter we look at:

- What is a mild learning disability?

- What are the effects on the individual?

- What are the implications for parenting?

- Predictive factors.

- Issues in engaging with families.

- Working and communicating with people who have mild learning disabilities.

What is a mild learning disability?

In Chapter 1 we have seen that a learning disability is determined by three main factors:

1. intellectual functioning, which refers to general mental capacity and is usually assessed by an IQ test

2. adaptive behaviour and social functioning – the collection of conceptual, social and practical skills and behaviours that are learned and used by people in their everyday lives

3. age of onset – there is evidence of the disability during the developmental period, usually thought of as occurring before the age of 18.

It is important to emphasize that there are three elements to the diagnostic description; sometimes people focus on the IQ score alone, which may result in a skewed understanding of the person and inappropriate expectations of what she is able to achieve.

IQ tests and their interpretation

Intellectual functioning, or cognitive ability, is usually measured by individually administered tests which are psychometrically sound and valid. In other words, they are recognized by those in the field to be effective, based in current theory and useable. These tests are used and interpreted by appropriately qualified and specialized psychologists (e.g. clinical and educational psychologists). Where a parent has a suspected learning disability, best practice indicates that any diagnostic assessment should be carried out by a psychologist with a specific speciality and clinical experience in learning disabilities.

The most commonly used and well-recognized tests are the Wechsler group of tests – the Wechsler Adult Intelligence Scale (WAIS) and the Wechsler Intelligence Scale for Children (WISC) for school-age test-takers – although other tests may be used. These tests have a mean, or average, of 100 with most of the population scoring within the 'average' category.

People with mild learning disability would be expected to score between 55 and 70, with a margin for measurement error (day-to-day variation) which is generally plus or minus five points. Scores with this measurement error added are sometimes quoted as 'confidence limits'. This recognizes that there is likely to be some variation in scores and the confidence limits give you the upper and lower range of that variation.

We can see by looking at the predicted IQ population distribution in Figure 2.1 that 2.1% of the population would be expected to have mild learning disabilities. Added to this figure are a suggested additional unspecified number of people suffering from early deprivation which has served to limit their cognitive potential.

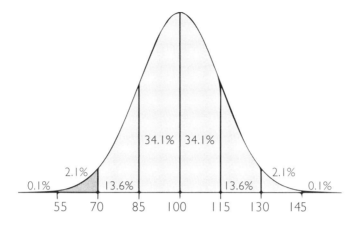

Figure 2.1 Normalized IQ distribution with mean 100 indicating expected population with mild learning disabilities

Factors which may affect test scores include:

- practice effects: if you have done the test recently, you may be more prepared with an answer (it is not recommended to repeat testing within 6–12 months for this reason)

- the 'Flynn effect': this describes the overall effect of test scores improving over time, and means that up to date versions of tests and norms must be used in both the administration and interpretation of IQ assessments

- socio-cultural background and native language: appropriate norms must be used

- co-occurring disorders affecting communication or motor function: test selection and interpretation must take account of such difficulties.

Adaptive behaviour

Assessment in this area involves three domains – conceptual, social and practical – covering a wide range of behaviours and skills. Each person's profile of strengths and difficulties in adaptive behaviour will be different; however, general trends can be identified.

The *conceptual* domain involves skills we might think of as 'academic' – memory, language, reading, writing, number skills, knowledge acquisition, problem solving and the ability to make reasoned judgements. People with mild learning disabilities will require support with learning academic skills. Abstract thinking and the group of cognitive processes known as executive functioning (forward planning, problem solving, flexible thinking and priority setting) will be impaired; as a result, approaches to problems tend to be concrete and limited in adaptability. Short-term memory is likely to be poorer than average, and functional use of academic skills in tasks such as literacy and money management is restricted.

The *social* domain focusses more on socially based behaviour and skills – empathy, interpersonal relationships, management of relationships, social behaviour and responses, communication and emotional behaviour. In people with mild learning disabilities, communication, conversation and language are immature and likely to be concrete. Interpreting social cues and the regulation of social behaviour is less well developed than that of their peers; the effect of this is to limit both the ability to understand risk in social situations and the ability to make sound social judgements. The person is at risk of being exploited or manipulated by others with more sophisticated social behaviour.

The *practical* domain looks at a range of practical personal and life management skills – time management, money management, self-care, household care, recreation and community involvements. People with mild learning disabilities would be expected to manage personal care and the basic activities of daily living. The repertoire of skills will depend on experience and opportunity; for example, was the person brought up in a household where positive examples and teaching were available? It may be that low levels of skills in this area simply reflect family standards, or they may indicate a lack of opportunities to learn and practise a range of life skills. This is not an exhaustive list, but gives broad examples of what might be assessed.

Adaptive functioning may be assessed by clinical evaluation and by individualized, psychometric measures. These psychometric measures are used with an appropriate informant and/or the individual. The problem with these measures is that over- or under-reporting may skew the results. It is usually best to compare results with observed behaviour and corroborate with additional sources of information such as educational or medical evaluations.

In order to meet the criteria for diagnosis, difficulties with at least one of the three adaptive behaviour domains will be evident.

Age of onset

The onset of learning disability is during the developmental period: before age 18. That is, problems with development and progress through early milestones and education will have been noticed, even if a formal diagnosis had not been made. A more general diagnosis of 'global developmental delay' may have been suggested, or a condition such as ASD or attention deficit hyperactivity disorder (ADHD) which partially explains any observed delay.

What are the effects on the individual?

Learning disability is often referred to as a heterogeneous condition, and one with many causes. This means that the group of people we refer to as having a learning disability is diverse. As with all of us, each person will be a mix of inherited, familial characteristics, her own personality, factors associated with environment and upbringing as well as any identified learning disability. This is why it is important to assess the whole person within her environment rather than just the 'disability'.

After childhood, a learning disability will be part of that person for the rest of her life. Levels of severity may change over time and the course may be affected by additional disorders such as epilepsy, sensory impairments or mental illness. A person with a learning disability is subject to the same range of experiences and developmental processes that affect us all (e.g. forming attachments and developing a sense of self and self-esteem). Some of these processes will progress in the same way as in the general population; some will have a subtly different course, influenced by the person's learning disability, which may affect adult behaviour and adjustment.

Developmental areas or processes that may be influenced by the person having a learning disability can be considered under four main headings:

1. social and emotional development

2. mental and physical health

3. personal cognitive profile

4. opportunities and experience life has offered.

Social and emotional development

Personal histories are all different, with a number of experiences and influences (both positive and negative) shaping our thoughts, feelings and behaviours. Early on, family reactions to a potential developmental delay are variable but tend to follow a similar pattern. It is usual for the family to grieve the loss of the 'normal' child whilst at the same time having to come to terms with disability, both emotionally and practically (Banks, 2003). The bereavement reaction follows the usual stages of initial numbness and shock, followed by overt grief and then the development of coping strategies. The extent and pace of this can vary from family to family; a lengthy adjustment period may affect the establishment of secure attachment between the primary caregivers and the child.

In the older child, communication difficulties and behavioural problems place stress on the family unit (Jacques, 2003); if the extent of the learning disability has not been recognized, the child can be put under pressure to achieve and even blamed for not cooperating or trying hard enough. Conditions often associated with learning disability, such as ADHD, ASD or other behavioural disorders, may emerge at this stage, complicating clear diagnosis and support pathways.

School-age children with learning disabilities, in comparison to typically developing children, report poorer emotional well-being, lower self-esteem and satisfaction in their personal relationships (Hollins and Foley, 2013), confirmed by social experience of rejection, bullying and scapegoating. At the same time, children with learning disabilities are more likely to have experienced abuse, neglect and exploitation and the accompanying emotional distress than the rest of the population (McGaw, Shaw and Beckley, 2007).

During adolescence, awareness of being different from peers and siblings affects self-concept. Although young people with learning disabilities have similar aspirations to young people without disabilities, a growing awareness of social barriers underpins potential development of social vulnerability and anxiety (Flynn and Russell, 2005). In adulthood, this awareness of the limiting effects of social barriers may crystallize into social exclusion, bringing problems of unemployment, insufficient skills, low income, poor housing, high crime rates, health concerns and breakdowns in support systems (Bonner, 2006). As vulnerable members of society, people with learning disabilities are particularly poorly equipped to deal with the effects of social exclusion and may experience anything from a poor quality of life to exploitation and harm.

Mental and physical health

The mental and physical health of people with a learning disability is influenced by the same factors that affect us all – lifestyle, familial health problems and environmental issues. In addition, further specific health problems may arise due to co-morbidity (i.e. the existence of other problems or risk factors in addition to the learning disability). Delays in recognition, diagnosis and appropriate treatment of health needs add to the overall poorer health status of people with a learning disability. 'Diagnostic overshadowing' – where the illness is attributed to the learning disability rather than diagnosed as a separate problem – continues to impact on recognition of illness.

Juliet's story

Juliet was a happy, smiley child; everyone loved Juliet, and when people realized that her development was slower than other children, she had plenty of people to look out for her. Aged 15, her parents separated and Juliet's life changed. She moved, with her mother, to another town and a new school; her mother was sad and quiet.

Juliet never saw her father again and didn't understand why. Juliet and her mother lived in an unhappy world. Juliet was quiet and often cried, but as her mother was like this too, she thought that this was what being older was like. Juliet had lots of developmental checks and reviews, but people in the new town just thought of her as quiet and shy.

Aged 18, Juliet moved into a supported residential placement. Her carer noticed that Juliet often cried, and began to ask about her mood. Juliet didn't know what to say at first because it was hard to describe, but she worked at finding words with her carer. Juliet went to see her GP accompanied by her carer and described how she was feeling. Her GP prescribed antidepressant medication, and Juliet found she cried less, was less tired and had more interest in her life. Juliet took the medication for six months, and is now slowly decreasing the dose with the help of her GP.

The Disability Rights Commission (2006) reports that people with learning disabilities are 58 times more likely to die before the age of 50. The main causes of mortality are respiratory and heart disease; people with learning disabilities are also more likely to have diabetes, sensory impairments, gastrointestinal disorders, obesity, dental problems, mental health problems or epilepsy. However, people with a learning disability have difficulty accessing primary care services (Emerson and Hatton, 2004). Health-related information is often written at a level which excludes those with poor literacy; people with learning disabilities may not have the telephone skills to explain symptoms and make appointments, and the services themselves are often not able to respond to the additional needs of clients in terms of allowing extra time and professional explanation. Research studies demonstrate that an estimated 25–40% of people with learning disabilities have mental health problems. The reasons offered for this include increased genetic and biological vulnerability as well as adverse life experiences such as institutionalization, separations, stigma and social exclusion.

Emerson and Hatton (2007) cite a prevalence rate of 36% for a diagnosable psychiatric disorder in children and adolescents with learning disabilities, as compared with 8% for the non-learning-disabled population. It further comments that these children and young adults were 33 times more likely to be on the autism spectrum, and more likely to have emotional and conduct disorders. Long-term health problems and disabilities such as epilepsy and sensory impairments were reported at a high frequency.

Cognitive profile

Fundamental features associated with learning disability are problems with learning and thinking skills. Even before a learning disability is diagnosed, slow development or difficulty in learning age-appropriate skills are likely to have been noticed. This will affect skill acquisition in all areas of life, such as literacy, self-care and communication. Overall problems with learning include:

- non-strategic approaches to learning (difficulty organizing information into meaningful segments, such as grouping or classification)

- problems with generalization of skills (transferring learning from one situation to different situations)

- difficulties with information processing (faulty links in the input, processing, integration, storage and output chain when working with information)

- limited social understanding (affecting relationships with others and the management and regulation of relationships)

- an overall slow speed of learning

- difficulties with managing the flow of information required in order to respond to sudden or new situations (problem solving)

- because of the extra effort involved in managing these processes, learning, decision making and complex thinking will be demanding and potentially exhausting and draining

- executive functioning (the theoretical cognitive system which synthesizes and manages other cognitive processes) may be impaired, implying difficulties in emotional regulation and self-monitoring.

(Nader-Grosbois, 2007)

The diverse nature of learning disability means that each person will have her own profile of strengths and limitations – a mix of some or all of the above, occurring with varying levels of severity. This highlights the need for individualized, careful and accurate assessment in order to begin to understand where a person's particular strengths and needs lie.

These cognitive difficulties, when combined with the social and emotional factors outlined above, bring a tendency for the person with a learning disability to view herself as having low competence, as other people seem to be so much more successful than she is. This increases suggestibility and persuadability so that social pressure is more effective. This social pressure may be positive – by coaxing, encouragement or inducement – or negative – using criticism, disapproval or threats, with the overall effect of intensifying personal vulnerability to exploitation.

Ian's story

Ian was a young man with a mild learning disability. He had gone to school at a local academy and so had lots of friends living near him. Ian's girlfriend was local too and expecting their first baby. Ian and his girlfriend were saving to buy things for the new baby – Ian told his friends proudly that they had enough money saved for a brand new buggy. One of Ian's friends asked to borrow £50, just for a day or two, until his benefits came in. Ian lent his friend the money, but heard nothing for the next two weeks. Ian saw his friend drinking in a pub and went in to ask him about the money. His friend said, 'Oh sorry, Ian, I meant to pay you back, here's the tenner I borrowed.' Ian told him it was £50 not £10, but the friend said Ian had got it wrong, remarking to other people in the pub that Ian was 'not quite right in the head'. Ian left as he wasn't sure now how much he had lent his friend, and didn't know what to do.

There has long been a link made between learning disability and locus of control. The term *locus of control* refers to beliefs about whether the outcomes of our actions are a result of what we do (internal control) or of events outside our personal control (external control). People who have external models believe events or outcomes are contingent on factors beyond their control (chance, fate, luck, bias or prejudice). Recent discussion on this topic has identified methodological limitations of early studies; current thinking suggests that a trend towards greater externalization is observed in children with a learning disability, and although this is mitigated with age (as in the general population), greater externalization remains evident (Shogren *et al.*, 2010).

Opportunities

Current government policies and service provision aim to empower people with learning disabilities to have access to the same things in their lives as we all expect – work, leisure, partners, a sense of being part of a social group and of being useful and valued. However, this is balanced against an adverse financial climate, affecting jobs, leisure provision and social care funding generally.

In childhood, education may be provided in the mainstream or special education sector. Difficulties may not be identified early, or appropriate support not provided, leaving a student struggling with the learning process, raising the risk of opting out of learning or even not attending school. Education within the specialized sector, whilst it should meet the child's specific educational needs, emphasizes difference as the child (usually) travels to a non-local school, potentially separating her from her local community. During adolescence, separation in education can compound social difficulties (attending a separate school, away from the local community or a special educational unit). Late diagnosis and limited support options will limit learning opportunities still further.

There is an increased likelihood of children with learning disabilities going into care or specialist units, some experiencing multiple placements. Leaving the parental home when the child has grown up at home usually occurs later in the life of someone who has a learning disability, with parents battling the wish to protect and overprotect. As a result, many young adults with a learning disability have not handled money, are not used to taking responsibility for household chores and have limited knowledge with respect to the processes of running their own home. Employment opportunities are restricted; in a competitive jobs market which increasingly demands paper qualifications, young adults with learning disabilities are easy to overlook. Young people with learning disabilities are less likely than their peers to gain paid employment.

Baurain and Nader-Grosbois (2013) explored the community participation of people with mild learning disabilities. They reported that people with mild learning disabilities were less likely to participate in decision making (including voting) and had less interaction with the community than the general population, confirming the relative social isolation noted in previous studies. The opportunity to take part in, and gain life experience from, meaningful activity is restricted; parental or carer overprotection contributes further to this restriction.

Bullying and hate crime against people with learning disabilities have been highlighted as a significant problem. A survey conducted by Mencap in 2007 revealed that eight out of ten (82%) children with a learning disability reported being bullied and 79% reported being scared to go out because they were frightened they might be bullied. This situation continues into adulthood, with the organization Disability Hate Crime (DHC) reporting 90% of people with learning disabilities in the UK said they had been bullied or harassed in the previous 12 months.

What are the implications for parenting?

Parents with learning disabilities share many factors in common with the general population. That is, parents in this group will have a range of skills and experiences, will aspire to be a good parent, to love and care for their children, and to be able to change their behaviour, and will have an individual response to the experience of being a parent. They will be aware of both the challenges and the satisfaction which being a parent brings. It is recognized in the UK that parents with learning disabilities can be successful, safe and good parents when provided with appropriate support, but, at the same time, parents with learning disabilities are disproportionately represented in care proceedings. Research shows that they are more likely to be involved in child protection investigations, be subject to a care application and lose care of their children than any other group of parents (Booth, Booth and McConnell, 2005).

It is unarguable that difficulties associated with a learning disability impact on the kinds of skills a parent needs to acquire. Knowledge of which potential areas are likely to be affected is critical to the setting up of any assessment and subsequent support plan as it allows those working with parents to be prepared and proactive in mitigating these difficulties. For these reasons, it is useful to explore how and why having a learning disability impacts on the role, task and functions of child care for a parent with a learning disability,

It is well recognized that families with a physically disabled or learning disabled child are economically and socially disadvantaged, with pressure on parents leading to relationship difficulties and the demands of care limiting employment options for parents. So disadvantages are intergenerational – likely to have been present from the parent's own childhood – and are continued into adulthood. In addition, parents with a learning disability have been shown to be more likely to have experienced poor parenting themselves, and so have limited internal models to draw on as a parent (Baum, Gray and Stevens, 2011).

During adolescence, one of the main developmental tasks is to prepare us for life as an adult. In order to do this, we experiment with relationships, learn about the world from a huge variety of sources, have a peer group for reference, feedback and discussion, and learn work skills such as listening, remembering and concentration through formal education. Moving into independent life presents a challenge to any adolescent; the young adult with learning disabilities will have more limited experience and opportunities for learning and gaining skills which significantly increases this challenge.

Many young adults with learning disabilities articulate their future wish to find a partner and establish a family, yet they often leave school with poor transition to adult services and become effectively 'lost' until referred by the midwife or health visitor (McGaw and Newman, 2005). At this point, the multiple stresses of managing housing, finance, a relationship and a new baby presents a huge set of demands to the individual who is likely to have a limited amount of knowledge about negotiating the new roles of adult and parent thrust upon her.

We know that, for a parent with a learning disability, everyday life is often experienced as demanding with a range of tasks which are hard to learn and remember. In general, the message received is one of not being good enough and it is not surprising that low self-esteem and a poor sense of personal efficacy often go hand in hand with a learning disability. Lamont and Bromfield (2009) comment on families with parents who have a learning disability as likely to have low socio-economic status and live in social isolation – all of which impact on their coping abilities as parents. As early as 1998, Llewellyn *et al.* reported parents with learning disabilities as voicing the need for help with making friends and social and community contact generally. Mothers with learning disabilities report an average of four or five central people who were either family, professionals or friends (Guinea, 2001). When they investigated support networks further, Llewellyn and McConnell (2002) found that single mothers tended to have service-centred networks; mothers with a partner had ore family networks (but these were not necessarily locally based family members) and mothers living with a parent were more likely to have local family networks. Supportive links with friends or neighbours were not often identified. The conclusions of this study highlighted the vulnerability of parents in the event of family breakdown, given the limited variation in community-based support links.

Predictive factors

With the recognition that the numbers of parents with a learning disability on social work caseloads is increasing and that this same group of parents is disproportionately represented in care proceedings, one focus of research has been to identify the factors that are associated with greater parental difficulty.

There is general agreement amongst researchers that when IQ falls below the level of around 60 (the 'around' allows for individual variation), the likelihood of successful parenting is significantly reduced (McGaw and Newman, 2005; Tymchuk, 1992b). This is because the new skills, rate of learning, ability to manage a number of tasks and decisions, and complexity of judgements needed as a parent require a level of cognitive competence less likely to be available to people with IQs at this level.

However, above this score level, research does not support a direct link between IQ scores and neglectful or abusive parenting. Evidence suggests that children suffer from neglect due to errors of omission rather than due to direct actions by the parents themselves. Often this is the result of a lack of parental knowledge and experience as well as a lack of supportive services (McGaw and Newman, 2005). The parents' resources, knowledge and skills may not match the child's needs; limitations in the support network (whether friends, family, community or statutory) mean that additional support and learning opportunities are not available or accessible.

Annie and Adam's story

Annie and Adam met at college. Annie had a mild learning disability and Adam ADHD. They moved into a flat together for three years before they planned their first baby. Adam was good at cooking and money; Annie preferred to do the washing and cleaning. They went shopping together. Adam's mum and dad often came round and helped with things like decorating and giving them lifts to appointments. Annie's mum helped by buying them furniture for the flat and often took Annie out for coffee. When Annie was pregnant, she had a social worker (through her midwife). Annie was scared the baby would be taken from her, but Adam, his mum and dad and Annie's mum said they would all work together with the social worker and plan how to care for the baby. Annie and Adam agreed to live with Adam's parents when the baby was born. Adam's mum would help them to learn how to look after the baby. Adam and Annie enrolled at a parents' class with the help of the social worker to learn more about being a parent. Annie and Adam had a baby boy and lived with Adam's parents for three months. They have moved back to the flat, but have regular visits from their parents and Annie phones her mum or Adam's mum if she needs advice. They often stay with Adam's parents for the weekend. So far, things are going well.

Cleaver and Nicholson (2007) point out that family stressors will have more effect on care than the parents' cognitive abilities, citing typical stressors such as a large number of children, marital conflict or violence, poor mental health, a history of abuse, substance misuse and social isolation and poverty. They add that parents with learning disabilities, because of their increased vulnerability, are more likely to experience multiple stressors and as a result are likely to experience high levels of stress. We have seen that people with learning disabilities are particularly susceptible to early emotional difficulties relating to attachment, low self-esteem, school experience and vulnerability to exploitation and abuse; these are all potential sources of pressure and will contribute to high stress levels.

Social isolation and poverty are much explored in the literature. A raised level of stress in parents with a learning disability had been shown to be linked with poor social support (Feldman, 2002), with consequent negative effect on parenting style. Aunos, Goupil and Feldman (2004) discuss a model of parenting for parents with a learning disability that assesses the cumulative risks of the personal and environmental factors present. The implication is that the higher the number of risk factors, the higher the potential risk.

McGaw, Scully and Prichard (2010) examined familial and demographic factors in mothers with learning disabilities and identified key elements associated with high-risk parenting. Their study concluded that the key risk factors were:

- *Mothers with a learning disability and a history of early trauma (particularly emotional abuse and physical neglect)*: this accords with mainstream research which emphasizes the increased emotional vulnerability of parents with a history of childhood abuse (Schuetze and Eiden, 2005) and the link between the experience of childhood physical abuse and a raised risk of becoming a physically abusive parent (Narang and Contreras, 2005).

- *Mothers with a learning disability and additional needs (particularly physical or sensory disability)*: co-morbidity (the existence of one problem with another) has often been signalled as a potential problem area by researchers. Other studies have highlighted psychiatric rather than physical or sensory co-morbidity as a significant contributory factor (Goodinge, 2000).

- *Mothers with a learning disability whose child had additional needs*: the children of parents with a learning disability have an increased risk of inheriting psychological and physiological difficulties (McGaw and Newman, 2005). We know that parents generally struggle in the task of parenting a child with special needs; parents with learning difficulty appear to find this struggle particularly challenging, with a consequent effect on parenting.

- *Mothers with a learning disability whose partner had a history of criminal or antisocial behaviour*: this finding emphasizes the vulnerability of mothers in their choice of partner – the partner may bring strengths to the relationship, but this is undermined by the complications of their negative behaviour.

- *Mothers with a learning disability whose partner did not have a learning disability*: this is a limited finding, although it confirms the direction of earlier studies, that where a partner has a higher IQ than the mother, particularly when the partner does not have a learning disability, outcomes may be poorer. The reasons why this may be are not yet fully explored, but an initial hypothesis seems to be that parents are likely to be more compatible when both parents have a learning disability; this is associated with less risk to the children. Partnerships where mothers have a learning disability and the father does not may reflect the mother's vulnerability in her choice of partners. However, the authors also recognized that male partners who did not have a learning disability could bring many positives to the relationship.

Issues in engaging with families

Positive engagement with families is an important part of both the assessment and support process whatever the diagnosis of the parent(s). Howe (2008) comments that for working relationships to be successful, engagement must be at an emotional as well as a professional level. The first task when beginning to work with families, and often an overlooked step, is to consider how your relationship with the family will both work well and prove productive.

Commonly cited difficulties for families where either or both parents have a learning disability can be related (at least in part) to the nature of the relationship established between the family and their main worker. Parents who feel constantly monitored and over-assessed, treated like a child, overwhelmed by the support process itself and working to impossibly high standards (Booth, Booth and McConnell, 2005) are unlikely to feel that they have established a working partnership with their main worker. At the same time, social workers, in particular, have to negotiate the dual role of supporter and assessor.

A Swedish survey (Starke, 2010) of seven mothers with a learning disability reported three consistent themes running through their results. The first two themes can be allied to engagement as they were about the parent's need to understand and accept that she would benefit from support; in addition, parents needed to see that the support offered was the right support for their family. Information and discussion needed to be presented in a timely and accessible manner: one that met the family's perceived requirements. The end result of this was expressed in the third theme from this research which was that some of the mothers felt empowered when the support offered met their needs.

Some parents will already be asking for support and will engage successfully with services when they are discussed and offered. Some parents, however, will be much more difficult to engage and display a range of delaying tactics, excuses, avoidance or outright hostility, which effectively blocks progress.

Help-seeking models suggest that support seeking is triggered by perception of need (Cohen, 1999). The simple explanation is that parents with a learning disability do not understand what is required in the situation, see accepting support as an admission of failure or are frightened of having their children removed from their care. These explanations may be partly true, but the complete picture is likely to be much more complex. We need to consider all the elements in operation, including understanding the interaction between the parent's learning disability and the engagement task.

In common with most parents, parents with learning disabilities prefer to be supported by members of their informal network rather than by professionals (Llewellyn and McConnell, 2002). In a study exploring support-seeking behaviour, Meppelder *et al.* (2014) found that parents with learning disabilities took longer to seek support from professionals than from an informal support. They also found that a good informal support network may well delay support seeking from professionals, even if relationships with professionals were positive. Overall, positive working relationships with professionals accelerated support seeking. The authors concluded that before automatically considering low support seeking as a risk, parental support networks should be reviewed with these points in mind. They highlighted that parents with small support networks may need to be approached proactively and actively encouraged to seek support.

Negative emotions relating to the support process

Earlier in this chapter, we have seen that, for a parent with a learning disability, everyday life is demanding; being a parent requires knowledge and experience which may be lacking or difficult to access. Parents may feel not good enough, which compounds potentially already low self-esteem. The economic and social disadvantages of being a parent with a learning disability are well documented, as are the potential emotional difficulties.

These factors are likely to be present to a greater or lesser extent in all parents with learning disabilities. Some parents will be able to balance these with positive experience and attributes, but, in others, these factors will combine to generate negative emotion – not necessarily to being a parent, but to the whole process surrounding the parenting-assessment-support experience.

The idea that another person (a stranger) can come into your home and effectively dictate the future of yourself, your family and your child can be highly antagonistic. Even if handled sensitively and carefully, strong reactions are provoked and sometimes exacerbated by members of the extended family. As a parent, your role is to bring up your child. Having another voice in the matter – and a voice which must be attended to – is likely to generate a level of frustration and fear. Already aware of society's negative view of parents with a learning disability, parents approach services with hostility and an awareness of the imbalance of power (Traustadottir and Sigurjonsdottir, 2010). The expression of these negative emotions may be:

- anger

- disdain or dislike

- fear and sadness

- confusion.

All of these serve to inhibit the engagement process.

Bringing ideas on the working alliance (Bordin, 1979) which is formed between professionals and parents is helpful when considering engagement. Here, the critical factors are the quality and nature of the interaction between parent and professional, the level of agreement about the intervention's aims, goals and tasks, and the bond or connection between participants which results.

When working with parents with a learning disability, interactions must take account of language and communication needs. Advice that is contradictory (different professionals giving slightly different advice on the same topic) has the potential to raise anxiety levels in the parent who is trying her best to follow the instructions of professionals, as does over-complicated advice. When complexity levels are too high, the risk is that parents will not ask for explanation in case they are seen as lacking competence, adding to the confusion created by a lack of clarity (Traustadottir and Sigurjonsdottir, 2010). Interactions with parents must also be sensitive to the potential vulnerabilities (a history of abuse, social exclusion, mental health difficulties) outlined earlier, and the complexities which this may add to the working partnership.

Agreement about aims, goals and tasks can help to address power imbalance in the relationship between parent and professional. Advice that is not consistent with the parents' own values may not be followed, or incorporated only briefly into the parents' repertoire (Traustadottir and Sigurjonsdottir, 2010).

Establishing a positive connection between professional and parent fulfils Howe's requirement for engagement to be at an emotional as well as a professional level (Howe, 2008). A positive, containing relationship will allow feelings of anger, sadness or confusion to be expressed directly and reasonably, helping to defuse unexpressed emotions. If not recognized or addressed, these feelings can also build into a sense of antagonism and resentment, which will clearly hinder any joint working relationship you are trying to foster.

Rose's story

Rose had a three-year-old girl, Skye. The last few times she had collected Skye from nursery, the manager had taken Rose to one side and told her that she was worried that Skye did not look very clean. The manager said that she had contacted social services about this, and someone would probably visit her to talk about Skye. Rose was very worried and confused. She felt she was doing her best, but getting Skye ready in the morning was sometimes very difficult. Rose went round to her auntie's to talk about this; her auntie scared Rose even more by saying that she shouldn't trust anyone from 'the social' because they would want to know all about her. Rose had a letter telling her that she would be visited by a social worker. Rose was so frightened she threw the letter in the bin and pretended it had not arrived. Luckily, Rose's assigned social worker found Rose in. She took time to explain to Rose why she was there, and talked about the sort of help Rose might need. The social worker did not use any big words that Rose didn't understand, and didn't make Rose feel stupid. Rose decided that, in spite of what her auntie had said, she could trust this person and looked forward to seeing her again.

Working and communicating with people who have mild learning disabilities

Professionals do play an important role in the lives of many parents with learning disabilities. Their role and input are likely to make a critical difference in the family's future. Many parents with learning disabilities will not have had contact with their local learning disability services as their potential support needs may not be recognized by mainstream services (Green and Vetere, 2002), or, when referred, they do not meet eligibility criteria until they are in crisis. If referred at crisis point, often it is too late for specialist support and interventions to be implemented, and the family moves into formal proceedings.

Ward and Tarleton (2007) mapped areas of positive practice in working with parents with learning disabilities. They commented on the enthusiasm and commitment of both professionals and services found during the course of their research.

They and other researchers highlight that in order to inform appropriate support, assessment should:

- be holistic
- be contextually based
- assess parents' existing skills (Ward and Tarleton, 2007)
- work to an interagency plan to avoid duplicating assessment
- include fathers and other males who make a contribution to or influence the family (McGaw and Newman, 2005).

Assessment may take the form of formal, specialist evaluations (such as by a speech and language therapist), more generalized assessment specific to parents with learning disabilities (such as the Parent Assessment Manual; McGaw *et al.*, 1998), joint assessments between learning disability professionals and children's services, community care assessments, home visits and informal 'getting to know you' exercises with parents.

Butler-Sloss (1988) reminds us of the intrusions into family life which the assessment process makes and that over-assessment can be counterproductive as the assessment process loses focus and ethical questions are raised.

Interventions

In general, research evidence suggests that parenting skills can be improved with appropriate support, although comparing studies is difficult as samples tend to be small, there is variability in the level of learning disability of parents participating in the programmes compared and studies to date are of mixed quality.

Research into interventions used focusses on two principal areas: teaching parenting skills and establishing or consolidating social behaviours and relationships (IASSID, 2008). Teaching skills clearly relates to parenting behaviour and knowledge, whilst strengthening social behaviour and networks has an effect on psychological well-being and hence an indirect effect on parenting behaviour. The key points of this research can be summarized as follows:

Research into skill teaching:

- An early review suggested that focussing on performance (doing things) rather than a knowledge-based (knowing things) approach improved outcomes.

- Adopting a behavioural approach using praise, feedback and breaking down tasks into their constituent parts improved learning outcomes (Feldman, 1994).

- Parental perception of support as relevant is critical in order for that support to be viewed as positive (Aunos, Goupil and Feldman, 2004).

- This has been supported by later research; for example, behavioural-based parenting interventions were more effective than passive techniques such as information leaflets (Wilson *et al.*, 2012).

- In order for learning to be maintained, teaching must be long-term and consistent (Baum, Gray and Stevens, 2011).

- Programmes tailored to parents' specific needs, rather than generalized support, helps to improve learning and retention and home-based, intensive teaching was more successful than other, less concentrated interventions (Llewellyn *et al.*, 2003).

- Reasonable support for skills teaching methodology was found in a later review (Wade *et al.*, 2008). However, the authors noted the lack of information on the generalization of skills and the positive or negative influence of contextual factors.

- Recent reviews by Coren *et al.* (2011) and Wilson *et al.* (2013) highlight the status of research in the area of parent training for parents with a learning disability. Both used a database search returning a number studies, but few of these studies met rigorous inclusion criteria for review.

- Of the small number of studies which met the criteria for inclusion, the authors concluded that most of the studies supported improved parenting skills following a programme of training, although one recorded less definite results. However, they also note the small number of studies available for review and emphasize the need for further high-quality research.

Research into social relationship interventions:

- A semi-structured group setting was used to help improve self-concept and the quality of parents' relationships with others, using a cognitive behavioural approach and 'homework' activities. Parents attending the group showed improvement in both areas when compared with the control group, but this did not seem to have an additional effect on ratings of feelings about their children or perception of their children's behaviour and capabilities.

- This study also showed that parents who had previously attended groups were able to make bigger shifts in their attitudes and perceptions than those who had attended a single course (McGaw *et al.*, 2002).

- An evaluation of the Australian Supported Learning Programme indicated an overall reduction in psychological distress in participating mothers at the end of the course. This programme targets social relationships and psychological well-being using questioning, reflection, support and home tasks to work towards individual action plans.

- In their review of studies, Wilson *et al.* (2013) comment that research on social relationship interventions suffers from similar difficulties to those noted with respect to research into parenting skills teaching. Only two studies met their rigorous inclusion criteria, and even these presented design problems restricting the interpretation of their findings.

Three overarching difficulties relate to the body of research on parents with learning disabilities. First, it mostly concerns those who are in contact with social services – we know little about the experiences and support needs of families who do not have regular contact with social care. Second, the research focusses on parents of very young children, usually under-fives. This gives a skewed role of the parent and does not reflect, for example, the demands of parenting an adolescent. Third, the literature concentrates heavily on mothers. More generalized literature on learning disability tends to be genderless. This has meant that mothers with a learning disability have been bracketed with discussions on the experiences of women as mothers and childrearing, but the experiences of men with learning disabilities as fathers is largely absent from our body of knowledge. The majority of empirical studies have mothers with a learning disability as subjects, few refer to fathers and fewer still explore aspects of fatherhood in learning disabilities specifically. The support needs of mothers and fathers who have a learning disability may well be quite different, yet this remains an under explored area.

Summary

The main points of this chapter can be summarized as follows:

- Learning disability is a heterogeneous or highly diverse condition with many causes. Each person will have a mix of inherited, familial characteristics, her own personality, factors associated with environment and upbringing as well as any identified learning disability, which is why it is important to assess the whole person within their environment rather than just the 'disability'.

- A person with a learning disability is subject to the same range of experiences and developmental processes that affect us all. Some of these processes will progress in the same way as in the general population; some will have a different course, influenced by the person's learning disability, affecting adult behaviour and adjustment.

- Developmental areas or processes that may be influenced by the person having a learning disability are social and emotional development, mental and physical health, personal cognitive profile and opportunities and experience life has offered.

- It is recognized in the UK that parents with learning disabilities can be successful, safe and good parents when provided with appropriate support, but, at the same time, parents with learning disabilities are disproportionately represented in care proceedings.

- Knowledge of how any learning disability impacts on individuals is critical to the setting up of any assessment and subsequent support plan as it allows those working with parents to be prepared and proactive in mitigating these difficulties.

- Positive engagement with families is an important part of both the assessment and support process as commonly cited difficulties for families where either or both parents have a learning disability can be partly related to the nature of the relationship established between the family and their main worker.

- In general, research evidence suggests that parenting skills can be improved with appropriate support, although comparing studies is difficult as samples tend to be small, there is variability in the level of learning disability of parents participating in the programmes compared and studies to date are of mixed quality.

Chapter 3

Borderline Learning Disability and Parenting

In this chapter we look at:

- What is a borderline learning disability?
- What are the effects on the individual?
- What are the implications for parenting?
- Working with people who have borderline learning disabilities.

What is a borderline learning disability?

People who are described as having borderline learning disability (or this may be more generally described in their records as a 'learning difficulty') fall between two stools. Their cognitive abilities do not allow a label of 'learning disability', which – although some would regard this as a negative description – at least entitles the person to specific support and consideration. At the same time, they struggle to meet the requirements of everyday life unaided. Support services tend to be clustered and delivered to people with particular sets of problems: those with a learning disability or mental health problems. If your difficulties are hard to describe, generalized and vary with your circumstances, support tends to be ad hoc and very much dependent on the attitude of family, professionals and the accessibility of local services. In times of austerity, these 'local services' tend to be hard hit by city or county council cost savings.

Edgerton (2001) refers to a 'hidden majority' – those who may have been labelled as 'slow' during their school years, but as adults have coped in the community with little, if any, specialist support. Concern over their cognitive ability may only be raised once they become parents, as the multiple demands of parenthood highlight cognitive limitations and poor coping skills. To the average person, there is nothing to mark out the person with borderline learning disability as particularly different. As a consequence, the societal expectations of him are usually higher. And when he can't meet those expectations, society can blame him, or perhaps he even blames himself. People within this group may have been denied supports because it was mistakenly thought that they could do without them if they were sufficiently motivated. Or perhaps people within this group have rejected offers of support because they think that this will cause them to be stigmatized as 'disabled' or not coping.

Lee's story

Lee coped with primary school fairly well. He was always bottom of the class, with reports home highlighting his tendency to mess about in class and not attend. At secondary school, Lee found his schoolwork hard to understand. He didn't think about this; he just knew that when he was presented with a piece of work to complete, he did not understand. He felt bewildered, frustrated, ashamed and finally angry. Lee did not want to admit that he couldn't understand his work – a few of the kids had called him 'thick' already; instead, he began disrupting classes, with his frustration and shame giving way to anger. Lee was excluded from school many times and his attendance was poor; in his last year he hardly attended at all. Lee left school with no formal qualifications. He attended college, completing a Skills for Life course. This went better, as the college was able to pace work to the individual and support was available, but Lee did not enjoy the experience or see it as worthwhile because it reminded him of his schooldays. Lee soon dropped out and now avoids using his literacy and learning skills, which have not improved further. His self-esteem is low and job prospects are poor. Lee has a growing problem managing his anger, as he feels people are too ready to criticize him and put him down.

Lee's story is typical of many people with borderline learning disabilities. His early problems were not serious enough to be identified specifically – explanations like 'not attending' and 'not trying' are often applied. This happens when the behavioural problems, which have their root in frustration and lack of comprehension, dominate. Lee's story illustrates the possible early range of difficulties this can create with learning, self-concept and self-monitoring of behaviour.

Defining borderline learning disability

To understand this term we need to return to the diagnostic criteria of learning disability outlined in the previous chapters. The three key areas which need to be assessed for a diagnosis are:

1.   intellectual functioning

2. adaptive behaviour and social functioning

3. age of onset.

For a diagnosis of borderline learning disability, the assessment of intellectual functioning would indicate IQ scores between 70 and 80, or some clinicians use 70–85 – in other words – between the range indicating cognitive impairment and the 'average' range. The statistical distribution curve suggests that 13.6% of the population would be expected to lie within the IQ score range of 70–85, which includes a significant sector of the population (see Figure 3.1).

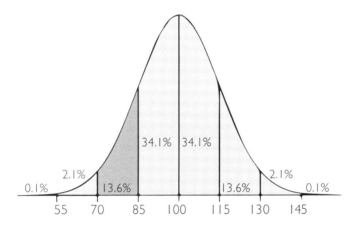

Figure 3.3 Normalized IQ distribution with mean 100 indicating
expected population with borderline learning disabilities

From a cognitive point of view, difficulties are likely to have been evident from school age – a primary indicator being academic failure or underachievement. Behavioural problems may also be a cue (as in the example of Lee) communicating the frustration triggered by being presented with situations or work which are confusing and hard to manage. Many schools will not have the resources to recognize, access guidance and provide support for pupils within this academic group. Instead, pupils leave school with, perhaps, a few low-grade qualifications, low self-esteem and a confirmed dislike of anything resembling a classroom situation.

Adaptive behaviour and social functioning will show mild impairments only. The person is likely to have a range of practical, everyday skills, be able to manage living in independent accommodation and have some, but limited, personal care, cooking, cleaning and community skills. More complicated activities, such as budgeting and managing housing difficulties may present greater problems because of their complex nature. There may well be current or past debts and difficulties with overall life management (e.g. prioritizing appointments or clearing accumulated clutter). In terms of social functioning, the person will probably manage normal social interactions and activities, but will find coping with and responding to unexpected or high-intensity social challenges more problematic.

Age of onset would remain as before the age of 18, although specific identification of any difficulties will vary with each individual. Where problems are milder, it is possible that difficulties passed unnoticed at school, especially if attendance was poor, or that difficulties were noted but not specifically assessed or quantified.

What are the effects on the individual?

Embedded in a borderline learning disability are likely to be specific problems with learning itself – that is, specific learning difficulties. *Specific learning difficulties* is a generalized term which covers a number of particular problems. Usually these difficulties become evident when a child struggles at school, but problems may not be identified, may be mis-identified or schools may lack the resources to meet specific learning needs. This begins a cycle of perceived failure, low self-confidence and poor self-esteem.

Specific learning difficulties

DYSLEXIA

Dyslexia is thought to be one of the most common specific learning disabilities, with about 1 in every 10–20 people in the UK having some degree of dyslexia. It seems to be more common in boys than girls and varies from mild to severe.

Dyslexia affects the ability to learn to read and spell. It involves difficulties in dealing with the sounds of words and can affect short-term memory. Someone who has dyslexia may either avoid reading and writing whenever possible or conceal difficulties with reading and writing from other people; he may also have poor spelling.

People with dyslexia have specific difficulties with the following:

- *Phonological awareness*: small units of sound, or phonemes, are basic building blocks in the development of sophisticated reading skills. Without this understanding, reading is limited to recognizing word shape, which means that only a relatively small number of words can be read and remembered accurately. The ability to blend phonemes together into words allows us to develop an ability to read an increasing number of complex and unfamiliar words.

- *Verbal memory*: remembering even short sequences of verbal information is difficult, such as a shopping list – 'eggs, milk and tomatoes' – or various instructions such as 'take this form, sign it and put it in the tray in the room next door'.

- *Verbal processing speed*: it takes extra time to recognize, process and produce a response to verbal information, resulting in a slow working pace, often with many mistakes.

- *Organizational skills*: managing everyday life, particularly time management, is difficult and the person may appear disorganized and chaotic.

DYSGRAPHIA

This is the term used for difficulties with written language, affecting the ability to recognize the shape of individual letters, to write letters and words or to link sounds with written letters or words. It is considered to be a problem linked with:

- fine motor skills

- visual integration of information

- motor memory and coordination.

People with dysgraphia have considerable difficulties with writing but may be wrongly judged as lacking in motivation. Tasks which to others may seem easy, such as making a list, require effort and the control of frustration and fatigue.

DYSCALCULIA

This is a general term for difficulties with number concepts. It affects understanding of such numerical ideas as quantity, place value and time as well as organizing numbers in memory. People with dyscalculia usually have poor mental arithmetic skills and may even find using a calculator difficult. It will affect such everyday activities as using a map or travelling to new places as they may have a limited sense of direction; from a financial point of view, estimating costs, adding and subtracting and checking change all present problems. Comprehension of budgets and financial planning is restricted, potentially leading to financial difficulties if no systematic approach is adopted.

DYSPRAXIA

Dyspraxia has many different names (developmental coordination disorder, motor learning difficulty, motor planning difficulty and apraxia of speech) all reflecting the fact that it is primarily a motor disorder with difficulties in planning and coordinating movement. People with dyspraxia may appear clumsy, with fine and/or gross motor skills affected. Commonly, people with dyspraxia may struggle with communication – pronouncing words and expressing themselves.

Writing is difficult and slow, sometimes accompanied by difficulties with reading and spelling. Their social skills tend to be immature; this may develop into social anxiety in adulthood. Life skills that require coordination and spatial organization are harder to acquire; for example, learning to drive may be difficult.

General cognitive function

People who have a borderline disability are a highly disparate group, with a range of difficulties in thinking and reasoning skills. Specific problems have been described, but we will now consider some of the key areas of more generalized cognitive function – attention, memory, organization and problem solving – and what this means for the individual.

ATTENTION

The process of attention allows us to focus on our immediate environment and prioritize areas which need concentration and effort. Attention is important in complex (sometimes called 'higher order') cognitive processes such as forward planning (as in thinking, 'Next week is half-term for the kids, I need to do X, Y and Z'), risk assessment ('When will it be safe to allow my daughter to cross the road on her own?') and self-monitoring ('I must stay calm and not shout at my son's naughty behaviour'). People with a lack of attentional control:

- have difficulty sustaining attention over time
- are easily distracted, either by thoughts or things in the immediate environment
- tend to give up easily
- miss details
- appear to have a careless attitude
- have difficulty managing two tasks at the same time to a good standard
- start, but have difficulty finishing tasks.

MEMORY

Memory problems are often linked with attentional difficulties. The ability to store and retrieve information allows us to make decisions, manage our lives and use experience to address problems. Psychologists talk about three main systems of memory:

1. *Immediate (sensory) memory*, which is very short-term storage, often just a few seconds, of the world around us.

2. *Short-term (working) memory*, which is temporary storage of current information; this information can be manipulated and moved into long-term memory.

3. *Long-term memory*, which, as the name suggests, is continuing storage of information over the longer term. This information can be accessed and used when required for information, decisions and social behaviour.

The likely kind of disruption to occur in people with borderline learning disabilities within memory processes are:

- *Overloading with too much information*: because people are not able to be selective about what needs to be remembered they try to store everything with the risk that they remember very little, or inaccurate details.

- *Information is not stored systematically*: this leads to inaccuracies and forgetting. Accessing information in the long-term memory may be a haphazard rather than an organized process; this then reduces the utility and efficiency of stored experience.

ORGANIZATION AND TIME MANAGEMENT

Personal organization and management of time are also very much linked with attention. People with poor attention will have difficulty deciding which activity or action is the most important and then further problems focussing on a specific task and avoiding distraction. This leads to a highly disorganized lifestyle; particular casualties are likely to be the everyday, rather boring tasks as they lack appeal. This is important because many basic tasks of running a home are just that – rather dull and unappealing, especially if left to pile up! The problem is if, for example, a room is not tidied on a regular basis, it quickly becomes a jumble of all sorts of things. Putting away two or three days' worth of stuff is a fairly straightforward sorting task. After one month the task has changed from simple putting away to a long and complex exercise in sorting, making judgements and prioritizing. Then it has become much more difficult for someone with borderline learning difficulties to plan what he is going to do. A kind of 'learned helplessness' sets in; then nothing is done, so the problem simply increases. It is important for those working with people who have borderline learning disabilities to be aware of the very real difference in demand between those relatively simple, small tasks and the complexity inherent in a big practical project. Complex tasks must be broken down into manageable parts and strategies applied to support people with organizing the resource that is their time.

John's story

John was diagnosed with ADHD when he was eight years old. He was prescribed Ritalin, which he hated taking; as soon as he was 18 and had the choice, he stopped his medication. Everybody has told him he would 'grow out of' his ADHD behaviour, so John hoped he had. John still had lots of problems managing his life. In his twenties, John had a son, Jason. Although he did not live with the mother, John enjoyed fortnightly contact with Jason, but often missed his contact time or arrived late. John was in danger of losing his contact time because of his unreliability. John usually put things he had to do in his phone, but he frequently forgot to charge it. John's support worker suggested that he used a different way of organizing himself such as a calendar, but John said he didn't like writing. John's support worker helped him work out a system of initial letters to show appointments with people, with a really big 'J' to show contacts with Jason. John crossed off each day before bed so he knew where he was and what he was doing the next day. Now John is mostly on time for his contacts with Jason and feels more in control of his life.

PROBLEM SOLVING

In problem solving, we are thinking of any situation where change or resolution is needed; the change or resolution could be an action, or it could be a change in thinking. Generating these solutions is the first part of the process – if the situation is misunderstood, or the individual has poor life experience, simply thinking of ideas about how to tackle a difficult situation presents a challenge. Supportive relationships are a source of advice, help and reassurance, but individuals with appropriate skills and knowledge are less likely to be found in the support networks of people with problem-solving difficulties. Poorly planned problem-solving or maladaptive coping strategies are more likely to be used by people with attentional difficulties (Young, 2005), who are also more likely to lack flexibility in applying potential solutions. A positive coping style will help the person adapt to the various challenges of his life; a dysfunctional coping style will lead to poor quality and unhelpful solutions to problems encountered, increasing rather than decreasing difficulties.

Emotional and behavioural responses

In addition to the difficulties with thinking and reasoning skills described above, a number of emotional and behavioural responses – impulsivity, difficulties with social behaviour, frustration and lack of self-esteem – will have a significant influence on the way individuals manage their lives. These are considered next.

IMPULSIVITY

Impulse control refers to the control of behaviour, speech and thought processes. People with poor impulse control say or do things without thinking them through and reviewing possible consequences. They can be seen as tactless and irritating, but can also land themselves in difficult situations (e.g. impulsively challenging someone to a fight). The focus tends to be on short-term rather than long-term rewards; having to wait or deal with delay appears aversive. Typical impulse control problems are associated with a lack of insight and poor consideration of consequences, or a tendency to take short-cuts and opt for the immediate reward. Reckless or unsafe behaviour or choices become more likely, with self-interest taking precedence over consideration for others.

DIFFICULTIES WITH SOCIAL BEHAVIOUR

People with borderline learning disabilities are likely to grow up thinking that they are 'different' from others in some way and perhaps not as worthwhile – particularly if they experienced rejection at home or bullying at school. Negotiating interpersonal relationships is a highly complex process, and for people with social difficulties relationships may not develop as expected. Low self-esteem and a history of bullying or rejection lead to difficulties with the formation of lasting, positive relationships. Instead, relationships may be volatile and susceptible to breakdown. A wish to be liked and belong to a peer group can result in individuals being vulnerable to exploitation, as can inappropriate self-disclosure.

Helping people with borderline learning disabilities who have social difficulties to become more aware of their social behaviour and promoting an understanding of the link between social behaviour and the perceptions of others enhance the ability to make and maintain positive interpersonal relationships. This, in turn, allows the person to build a secure and supportive social network which will help him function within the wider community.

FRUSTRATION

Frustration and anger are normal emotions which everyone experiences from time to time. The important feature about anger is that it is expressed in a way that is appropriate for the situation and that it triggers change or control rather than creating additional problems. There are many reasons people feel angry. People with borderline learning disabilities are particularly vulnerable in a number of situations. They may misunderstand comments, blame or advice and take what is said too personally or as an implied slight; anger may be expressed in preference to other emotions such as distress or fear; it may be a response to a lack of success – feeling hopeless and stupid when things go wrong builds into a sense of frustration or it may be the way they have learned to behave and react over the years, a coping strategy seen as successful because it distances others. Helping people to take time to understand their reactions of anger and/or frustration and think about other ways of behaving is a core part of learning to express these emotions more appropriately.

LACK OF SELF-ESTEEM

Self-esteem is an important personal factor which has an impact on almost everything we do. Self-esteem refers to the way we think and feel about ourselves. It develops over time from a very young age. Research shows that a child's self-esteem is closely linked with academic and social success. Children with borderline learning disabilities often spend many years at school feeling confused, discouraged and helpless. They make judgements about themselves, comparing their performance with their peers. As a result, they may label themselves negatively as 'stupid' or 'unpopular'; these personal judgements may be reinforced by bullying and critical feedback from adults (parents and teachers). Once a child has established low self-esteem, this can be very difficult to change. A cycle begins to form of low expectation, with consequent little effort resulting in poor performance, which reinforces low self-esteem. Without significant support, changes or specific input, low self-esteem continues into adulthood where it has been shown to be linked with a number of negative outcomes, such as depression, anger, anxiety, low mood and a restricted ability to manage stress (Silverstone and Salsali, 2003). Self-critical thinking accompanies the expectation of failure, and a repertoire of avoidant, passive or defensive behaviour or even self-punishment helps to maintain this negative pattern.

What are the implications for parenting?

Parents who have a borderline disability are, then, a group with very mixed characteristics, more likely to present with a spectrum of learning and emotional needs. These needs will interact, so it is important to consider the effect of one on the other. For example, whilst working at learning a specific skill ask, 'What is the emotional impact of this on the person?' Or, when considering emotional issues, such as anger, consider the learning implications.

Careful individual assessment will help to disentangle the cognitive and emotional elements of a parent's presentation. This may be complex and may require specialist assessment such as a psychological assessment.

A number of thinking and reasoning skill areas and emotional-behavioural responses have been highlighted as potential areas of concern. We go on to consider how these might affect the role of being a parent, with simple strategies which could be used to help structure any professional input and incorporated into regular family visits.

Attention

We have seen that people with attentional problems find sustaining attention difficult, are easily distracted and are likely to give up before a job is completed.

Sustaining attention is important in order to complete tasks that are not immediately highly rewarding, and there are many of these which form part of every parent's lives. Washing-up is an obvious example, but if you do not understand the importance of play and have difficulty interpreting your baby's responses, then playing with a baby may fall into this category. The person needs to learn to be able to suppress the urge to change focus and to continue and persist with the task at hand. Setting small, achievable goals (washing one draining board full or making baby smile once) is helpful and gives something to work towards. Goal setting is a recognized way of motivating people (Medlin and Green, 2009) and feedback with positive rewards is an integral part of this system. Achievement of a goal is in itself a strong reinforcer and increases the likelihood of occurrence of that behaviour.

Distractions are always present in a busy family household. Realistically, they cannot be kept to a minimum all the time, but for important activities steps such as turning off the TV, switching mobiles to silent (or, better still, leaving them in another room), moving to a quieter room and limiting visitors can be taken. So, for example, for a specific play session with a toddler, taking these steps allows concentration to be on the interaction with the child rather than elsewhere.

Building rewards into the process helps with persistence. Rewards need to be appropriate and needn't be complicated. Self-administered rewards such as a tea-break, a bath or watching a (short) favourite TV programme can all be used, or perhaps a partner can notice and provide the positive feedback. Utilize individual interests and try to introduce some variation and novelty (e.g. by joining a toy library, toys used for a play session can be exchanged).

Memory

As a parent, you become responsible for remembering things for yourself, but also for your children. This results in many more things to remember and bring into daily life. Health and educational requirements can be varied and complex; managing routines and combining the needs of several children can be a major exercise in attention and recall. Many of the suggestions on supporting memory in Chapter 8 will be relevant here. In people with borderline learning disabilities, problems are likely to arise when processes in any of the memory systems previously mentioned (immediate, short- and long-term memory) are interrupted.

Too much information and distractions will interfere with the early part of remembering; if someone is not sure what to attend to, then he may not store the important bits for later recall. Memory aids such as a diary, calendar, phone or tablet can be very helpful – this is dealt with in more detail in Chapter 8. If electronic aids are incorporated into a memory support system, make sure that these are used appropriately and do not become a distraction in themselves.

People can use various techniques for improving memory; these will not be reliant on a 'prop' such as a calendar, so will be more versatile. Strategies to support memory include:

- *Repetition*: repeating information several times over helps to establish the memory which will then be available for recall.

- *Using a visual image as a reminder of what has to be remembered*: sometimes more over-the-top images are most helpful – for example, imagining an enormous ear on top of the local hospital building to remember a child's hearing test.

- *Mnemonics can be used, but these must be kept very simple*: mnemonics help to reduce information and make it seem less overwhelming, so can be used to express an idea: for example, STD – stop, think, do something else as a behavioural reminder, or SSS – swimming, sports kit, sandwiches – a more practical version for school.

- *Systematic sequencing*: this is useful for finding lost items or refocussing after a distraction. It involves retracing your steps in an organized way and can be helped by using questions to prompt this – Where was I when I lost my place? What was I doing? Where did I start?

- *Lowering anxiety*: anxiety and the accompanying feelings of stress will interfere with memory. Simple strategies such as counting to five, taking a deep breath or repeating a positive statement such as 'Keep calm, I can do this' are all uncomplicated ways of reducing mild task-based anxiety.

Organization and time management

Life as a parent is complicated, with many things to remember and to organize. If there are specific concerns around the child, then parents will have to deal with a number of professional appointments as well as contact with supportive agencies. This all makes time management an important issue.

People with borderline learning disabilities will usually be able to tell the time and have at least a basic concept of time periods – morning and afternoon, hours and minutes, months and years. They may also be poor judges of passing time and have difficulty estimating how long things will take. The planning aspect of time management involves estimating, making choices and forward planning, all of which are complex and demanding mental activities.

A good place to start is to ask a parent how he plans. Does he, in fact, make plans? Are they written or carried in the head? Are they constantly interrupted? Does he manage to finish and get a sense of achievement, or does he never quite get there? This gives a baseline from which to work.

Then the next step is to establish a planning method. This would probably work best as a joint activity rather than the parent taking responsibility, at least initially. Planning involves the following:

- *Making a decision about what the parent wants to do*: is he planning one task ('Sort out my clothes') or a group of tasks ('What shall I do with the children at half-term?')?

- *Making a list of the activities or tasks involved*: with the clothes example, 'I want to gather up the clothes, sort them out and then do something with the sorted clothes.' For half-term it might be better to make a morning, afternoon, evening plan and fill this in to have on the wall, like a more detailed calendar. Meals could be included too if this seems like a good idea.

- *Ordering or prioritizing these activities*: some will naturally fall into place; the order is fairly obvious in the clothes example. It might go something like: take clothes out of wardrobe and collect from other rooms, make three piles (keep, throw, charity shop), throw clothes away from that pile, bag up those for the charity shop, put 'keep' clothes back in the wardrobe. This can be tailored to suit each household. In the half-term example, priorities might be hospital appointments or play schemes which have been booked for certain days; other activities can then be added.

- *Planning where and when jobs are done* (with a rough time estimate which could be as simple as 'short' and 'long' jobs): pinning somebody down to a specific day or time is a good idea; otherwise there is a risk that the whole timetable will remain theoretical. You might need to work jointly in the initial stages and gradually withdraw, or find someone in the family to help make sure it all happens.

- *Adding something for the parent which makes it worthwhile* is a good idea: a treat or telling someone who will then say 'well done'. If all the parent does is work hard at dull jobs and nobody notices, then the planning process is not likely to last long. Breaks, time to relax and rewards are all essential to ensure that planning will be used again and again.

Problem solving

Problem solving requires sequenced, organized thinking and the inhibition of impulsive actions, and uses memory and attention skills. Like forward planning, it is an example of complex thinking and can be draining and exhausting. Problem-solving strategies usually fall into two categories: problem-focussed and emotion-focussed (Frensch and Funke, 1995). Problem-focussed solutions are structured and involve:

- Identifying the problem: a specific definition including what you want out of it – for example, 'I am always late for school and my daughter misses lessons; I want to be on time.'

- Thinking of possible solutions to the problem: this is like a personal brainstorming session. D'Zurilla and Nezu (1999) suggest that the more ideas you can come up with, somewhere there will be a good idea and taking time to choose a solution leads to better solutions.

- Deciding which solution seems likely to be best.

- Trying that solution.

- Asking: did that work, and why (or why not)?

Emotion-focussed solutions help the individual manage his feelings by talking to a friend, seeking advice, using counselling or using some specific techniques such as relaxation.

Impulsivity

We have said that impulse control problems are associated with limited insight and a lack of consideration of consequences. The decision-making process is shortened or avoided, which potentially impairs the quality of the response. There is a focus on short-term over long-term rewards, and reckless or unsafe behaviour or choices become more likely. The main aim of work with people who have impulse control difficulties is to raise awareness of their behaviour and the need for self-monitoring. You could then consider introducing an approach which emphasizes stopping and thinking before taking any action. This is basically a simplified version of a behavioural or cognitive behavioural management plan. Some techniques which help rein in impulsive behaviour are as follows:

- Work on one area or behaviour at a time so that you have a chance of success.

- Simple behavioural contracts can be used – for example, 'I will discuss any purchase over £10 with my partner first' – but they must be reviewed regularly.

- Use responsibility – suggest the person you are working with takes charge of a specific area. It could be managing the household finances – working out a budget and making sure that it works – but should reflect the individual's skill set and give the opportunity for a sense of achievement and control.

- Some impulsive people benefit from joining classes which teach self-regulation such as relaxation, yoga or martial arts. Skills learned in classes can then be applied to everyday life.

- Encourage good nutrition and sleeping habits. Someone who is hungry, tired or on a sugar high will not be able to prioritize management of his behaviour.

- Brainstorm ideas for activities for diversion when feeling fidgety or disruptive – for example, going out for a walk, playing with a squeezy ball or playing an electronic game for a short while.

- Discuss possible areas of difficulty in his life in order to help build awareness of potential pitfalls and plan alternative strategies.

- Introduce the mantra 'stop, think, do' to remind the person to pause before acting or speaking.

Social behaviour

As a parent, management of social relationships is a key skill. Partner relationships must be negotiated and relationships with children, immediate and extended family, other parents, friends, neighbours, health and social care professionals and teaching staff will all impact on parenting behaviour. Difficulties with social relationships need a problem-solving approach; both emotionally based and problem-focussed solutions may apply (see the section on 'problem solving'). Attending a variety of community groups can help with social difficulties, although introducing the person to the group (so that he does not feel awkward) may have to be planned. If specific social difficulties are evident (such as poor understanding of personal space), one-to-one discussions and role play would be a first step, with social skills-focussed groups as a back-up where necessary.

Frustration and anger

Whilst frustration and anger are something we all experience, parents who regularly experience uncontained frustration and anger raise the risk of harm to themselves, their partner and their children. Unhelpful management strategies include the person who denies feeling angry and 'bottles everything up'.

However, their anger and frustration are expressed in other ways; they may appear in unexpected situations, or may be vented on helpless others (such as children). Alternatively, feelings of resentment build up and unexpectedly spill over in an uncontrolled way. A different but equally unhelpful management strategy is the person who has a low irritation threshold and freely expresses his anger and whose behavioural repertoire is likely to feature intimidation, provocation, impulsivity and poor self-management. Where levels of anger and frustration are severe, specialist support would be the option of choice. When anger and frustration are a concern, but have not yet reached a level where specialist help need to be sought, with guidance and support some useful steps can be considered:

- Help the individual begin to talk about his angry behaviour. If it is too difficult to talk about personal anger, you could begin by discussing a TV episode featuring anger (soaps are useful here!) and then move on to personal behaviour.

- Introduce some simple control techniques such as counting to ten, deep breathing, positive self-talk, a brisk walk or changing from angry thoughts to thinking about something pleasant.

- Suggest the individual tries a reality check – thinking about what is happening and asking whether it is really worth getting upset about.

- Some people believe that unexpressed anger is harmful, but, in fact, becoming angry stresses the nervous and cardio-vascular systems. Discuss other ways the person could express himself without becoming angry and practise these.

- Identify stressful times of the day and try to schedule in some 'me time' around then – or shortly after as a reward for coping.

- Try to identify the kind of things that are triggers for anger and then work out alternatives or ways around them.

- Anger may be a cover-up for other feelings – failure, shame or hurt. Think about why someone is angry and if there are other emotions mixed in.

- Look at overall lifestyle – is the person getting enough sleep, does he exercise, does life seem a dull grind, or are there relaxing or fun times too?

- Is there a friend or relative who will act as a 'mentor'– to listen to gripes, encourage positive action and be generally supportive on an everyday basis?

Sometimes simple strategies are helpful and can redirect what might have become a major problem. There will be times when simple strategies are not enough, however, and specialist support needs to be put in place.

Self-esteem

We have seen that problems with self-esteem are likely to begin early on in life, with messages about not being good enough being confirmed by experiences such as bullying, apparent failure at school and difficulties with social relationships. The negative messages continue into adulthood and may have a profound effect on the ability to manage the demands of adult life and on mental health. Building confidence and unpicking a lifetime's negative feedback is not an easy job, but small changes in thinking and behaving can have a cumulative effect. The following offers some ideas on how to begin to tackle low self-esteem:

- Help to emphasize personal strengths; everybody has something he can do well, whether it's playing with the children, telling jokes or helping people. Ask the person to start a 'things I do well' list and ask friends, family and professionals to add to it.

- Sometimes the people we see often bring our mood down. Establish with the person who is a positive contact and who is not and then work out ways of limiting contact with those people identified as negative. He may have to meet those negative people from time to time, but can at least be prepared for what they say.

- We are often kinder to others than we are to ourselves. Encourage people to give themselves a break! Ask them to think of how they would talk to a friend in a similar situation and give themselves the same advice.

- Practise saying 'no' in different situations, role-played or real. People with low self-esteem often find it difficult to assert themselves and may become overwhelmed with things to do. Saying no does not necessarily offend people, but sometimes it has to be tried to believe it.

- Together, plan some personal goals and some family activity goals. It might be going out for a walk once a week, or joining an exercise class, but it must be something motivating and enjoyable.

- Work with the person to ensure that expectations of themselves are reasonable rather than 'setting up to fail'.

- Identify self-critical thinking and together think of ways to stop and change the subject.

- Develop an individualized menu of self-care 'treats' such as a chocolate bar, scented bath or time on the Xbox. Treats from the list can be used to celebrate success or just to bolster confidence.

Sometimes it will not be enough to try to make simple changes to lifestyle and thinking. Professional therapy will help to identify the course of development of an individual's low self-esteem and maintenance factors. The emphasis will then be on making changes which promote greater confidence and acceptance of the self.

Lucy's story

Lucy had a difficult time when she was young. Her mum was depressed and her father, a long-distance lorry driver, was hardly ever there. Lucy was close to her Nan, but she died when Lucy was 11, leaving Lucy feeling alone and unloved. Lucy was severely bullied at the local secondary school as she couldn't keep up with the work; eventually, she stopped going to school altogether. In her head, Lucy decided she was unlovable and must be a bad person because nobody seemed to want her now her Nan had gone. In her late teens, Lucy met a man whilst she was out for a walk. He took her for a drink and was nice to her. Lucy agreed to have sex with him in his car and liked the attention. Lucy soon found she was pregnant and looked forward to having a baby of her own to love, and who would love her. However, Lucy found looking after her baby daughter difficult. When the baby cried, Lucy didn't know what to do, and felt panicky. It was hard work and she began to worry that the baby did not love her. Eventually, Lucy decided that she couldn't look after her baby and she was placed for adoption. Lucy felt that all this confirmed how hopeless she was. However, the social worker who had handled the adoption process realized that Lucy needed some form of activity and support. She put Lucy in contact with a community support group who involved her in voluntary work. Doing this work and talking to others in her work group made Lucy think that she wasn't alone and that people seemed to like her. She became friends with Liam; their friendship developed into a romantic relationship. Through talking to Liam, and being with him, Lucy gradually began to build her self-esteem. She hopes some day to start a family with Liam, and, supported by him, feels she will be a more confident parent.

Working with people who have borderline learning disabilities

Securing a joint working relationship with parents who have borderline learning disabilities is important as long-term progress and change will only be achieved by working towards shared aims and goals. Within this working relationship, mutual respect will be a key factor in helping to secure engagement. Being clear about your expectations and planning together will help this process. If you can make learning a positive, non-threatening experience, engagement will increase. Work in an organized manner so that messages are clear and can easily be repeated for reminders.

Plan and structure your presentation of information. If you are introducing a particular topic for discussion:

- Outline your objective or goal.

- Progress in a structured step-by-step manner.

- Refer to the objective as you go along.

- Review what you have covered at the end of the session in terms of the objective.

- Use this review as a prompt in memory aids offered or during future sessions.

- Be explicit about the learning process itself – learning how to learn (metacognition). Help the client understand that learning doesn't just happen; you need to approach a task systematically, planning, pacing and evaluating as you go.

Summary

The main points of this chapter can be summarized as follows:

- People with borderline learning disability may struggle to meet the requirements of everyday life unaided, but fall in the gap in service provision, between learning disability and mental health services.

- Statistically, 13% of the population would be expected to lie within the borderline learning-disabled range of scores, although some researchers suggest that social deprivation enlarges this figure considerably.

- Cognitive and emotional factors interact and a number of key areas of everyday functioning are potentially affected.

- A number of specific learning problems are also associated with this group, including dyslexia.

- Simple strategies for managing the problem areas highlighted can be included as part of regular contact with parents.

Chapter 4

Mental Health and Learning Disabilities

This chapter looks specifically at mental health problems in the context of learning disability. It includes:

- a brief overview of the topic, including some of the problems of diagnosis

- descriptions of the mental health problems that are most likely to be seen in people with a learning disability who are also parents

- discussion of how these problems are likely to present and how this affects parenting

- possible treatment approaches.

Introduction

The high rate of occurrence of mental health problems in the learning-disabled population has been highlighted by researchers since the 1930s. Since that time, estimates of the levels of mental health difficulties in this population have varied between 10 and 49% (Dodd and McGinnity, 2003; Smiley *et al.*, 2007). Studies suggest that people with learning disabilities:

- are likely to experience the same range of mental health disorders as everybody else

- are particularly vulnerable to the development of mental health disorders

- have increased vulnerability because of physical susceptibilities (genetic and biological) and adverse life experiences (stigma, abuse and social exclusion) (Emerson and Hatton, 2007)

- are more likely to develop low self-esteem and have limited coping skills, both of which are associated with the development of mental health disorders

- may be prescribed medication for a number of physical, neurological and psychiatric symptoms; the interactions of these medications should be carefully considered as they may contribute to mental health difficulties (RCN, 2010).

Diagnosis of mental health problems in learning disabilities is complex. One major factor in this is the idea of *diagnostic overshadowing* (Mason and Scior, 2004). Diagnostic overshadowing refers to the reluctance of mental health professionals (and others) to acknowledge mental health difficulties in people with learning disabilities. Instead, any observed problems are considered as part of the learning disability itself, which is used as an explanation for irrational or challenging behaviour, without considering other options.

Other studies comment that people with learning disabilities may under-report symptoms by hiding under a *cloak of competence*. This phrase was first coined by Edgerton (1967) to describe how a superficially appropriate social manner is used to minimize difficulties. However, other authors take exception to this description, regarding the idea that problems might be seemingly deliberately 'hidden' in this way as demeaning and stigmatizing (Lemay, 2012).

A further complication is introduced by the traditional separation between mental health and learning disability services. This separation of services limits access because people are usually clients of one or other service (or responsibility can sometimes be passed back and forth between the two). The use of shared knowledge is also limited by this division as professionals located in different places, each with their own pathways for access and treatment, are less likely to talk to each other. In the absence of agreed referral pathways, access to specialist treatment for people with learning disabilities is denied; although there is evidence of attempts at joint working, progress is slow (RCN, 2010).

There are a number of diagnoses which occur across the whole population, but are also more likely to occur when someone has a learning disability, so it is a good idea to have an awareness of what these terms mean and how they are likely to affect parenting. Having an additional diagnosis adds complexity to the whole parenting picture. You may need to seek a more accurate diagnosis, encourage the parent to access treatment or adapt parenting strategies to take specific problems into account. The explanations offered here are brief descriptions which outline basic current thinking on each condition. Colleagues in specialist mental health, learning disabilities and even more specialized services such as specific services for people with ASD will be able to give additional information and guidance.

The diagnostic process

Accurate diagnosis is the basis for good and effective treatment in mental health just as it is in physical health. However, in physical health, symptoms are often obvious and observable (e.g. as in a sore throat or broken leg) and can be confirmed by laboratory tests. Diagnosis of mental health problems usually relies heavily on self-report – someone's description of how she is thinking and feeling. It may be particularly difficult for a person with a learning disability to respond to questions such as 'How are you feeling?' or 'When was this?' and 'For how long?' for a number of reasons. Shyness, anxiety or simply not being used to expressing how you are feeling in words may get in the way of giving a good description. Sometimes it is difficult to think about subjects such as 'How are you feeling? Is it better or worse than yesterday? Is it better or worse than most people?' Reporting dates and times or time intervals is often hard to get right. Reports from significant others (a partner, family, friends, other professionals) can be helpful in corroborating or providing additional descriptive information, although this must be sensitively handled to ensure that the individual remains central to the diagnostic process. Historical notes (GP records, early social records) can be invaluable sources of forgotten information, but also take time to trace and access. The diagnosing clinician will be considering the following:

- observations of the person's behaviour, speech and general presentation

- relevant history, including (current) potential stressors

- symptoms seen in the general population

- additional behavioural equivalents of these symptoms (e.g. being unable to express panic, but suddenly running away)

- the developmental stage of the individual (as compared with the chronological age); this sometimes gives a different perspective of how we expect someone to behave.

These points will all be considered alongside any modifications that may need to be made to diagnostic criteria in order to accommodate the person's learning disability.

We now turn to describing the major groups of mental illness, consider how symptoms may present in a person with a learning disability and the overall effect this may have on parenting. This is not an exhaustive list of every mental illness listed in DSM-5, but more of an overview of common mental illnesses likely to be part of many parents' history.

Depression and mood disorders

In everyday life, the word 'depression' is used in many ways. It is an entirely normal reaction to feel sad when something bad has happened to you, or to experience a period of low mood when you are going through a difficult time (e.g. separation and divorce or illness). It passes over time and is not the same as a mood disorder.

Depressive disorder is a type of mood disorder which will have a significant effect on the person's ability to carry out their daily routine, to have satisfying personal relationships and, without treatment, may last for weeks, months or years.

Between 10% and 15% of people are likely to experience a major depressive episode at some point in their lives. Most people with depression will have some (at least five or six) of the following symptoms:

- feeling sad, anxious or empty most of the time

- feelings of hopelessness or pessimism

- feelings of guilt, worthlessness or helplessness, a loss of self-confidence

- a loss of interest or enjoyment in hobbies and activities that were once an important part of life, including sex

- decreased energy, a feeling of utter tiredness or being slowed down

- difficulty concentrating, remembering or making decisions

- insomnia, early morning waking or oversleeping

- feeling worse at a particular time each day, usually in the morning

- appetite and/or weight loss, or overeating and weight gain

- a generalized sense of not being able to cope

- thoughts of death or suicide, suicide attempts

- restlessness, irritability

- physical symptoms, headaches, pains or digestive problems that do not seem to improve with treatment

- avoiding other people.

Some less usual forms of depressive disorder have a slightly different range of symptoms, including:

- *psychotic depression*, which occurs when a severe depressive illness is accompanied by some form of psychosis, such as a break with reality, hallucinations and delusions

- *postnatal (postpartum) depression*, which is diagnosed if a new mother develops a major depressive episode within one month after delivery; it is estimated that 10–15% of women experience postpartum depression after giving birth

- *seasonal affective disorder (SAD)*, where depression is experienced during the winter and lifts during spring and summer

- *bipolar disorder*, also called manic-depressive illness, characterized by cyclical mood changes: severe highs (mania) and lows (depression).

Depression and learning disabilities

Depression is the most common mental disorder experienced by people with a learning disability; however, it can easily be overlooked. Communication difficulties may make it harder for the person to describe her feelings and fears and symptoms are often under-reported (Hurley, 2008).

People differ in the number of symptoms they have, how severe the symptoms are and how persistent the symptoms remain. For someone with a learning disability, there may be gradual or sudden changes in behaviour patterns and/or presentation. Hurley (2008) identifies three important symptoms which were useful in differentiating people with learning disabilities and depression: a sad mood, crying and a loss of pleasure and enjoyment in everyday activities. Aggression and impulsivity were also considered as potential markers for mood disorder. In general, it has been concluded that although people with a learning disability may not meet the 'standard' criteria for depression, features which occur in modest numbers should be monitored and consideration given to a positive diagnosis.

What are the implications for parents with learning disabilities and depression?

Maternal depression has been associated with a wide range of developmental difficulties for the child, including problems in social, emotional, temperamental and cognitive functioning in childhood, potentially extending into adolescence (Wagner, 2011).

The first year of a child's life is a particularly sensitive period; depression during this time increases the probability of negative outcomes for the child (Bagner *et al.*, 2010). Younger parents (aged 15 to 24 years), parents with a history of depression and parents from deprived areas have been found to be at the highest risk for depression (Davé *et al.*, 2010). Whilst no research yet provides definitive information on the effects of depression on parents with a learning disability, we know that they are more vulnerable to the development of mental health disorders, more likely to be living in a socially and economically disadvantaged situation, and more susceptible to psychological distress, isolation and abuse (O'Keeffe and O'Hara, 2008). These factors raise the likelihood of the development of symptoms of depression and the associated effects on child development. If you are supporting parents with learning disabilities, an important part of that role can be in helping to recognize, monitor and encourage discussion of symptoms of depression. Promoting access to appropriate treatment and helping parents negotiate the various treatment pathways operated by local services will ensure that treatment is both appropriate and as effective as possible.

Treatment options

For low-intensity depression (where few symptoms are reported), the treatment strategy may be simply monitoring, encouragement to join a social group or increase physical activity, whilst reviewing progress.

Where a greater number of symptoms are reported, treatment offered is usually antidepressant medication, talking therapy or a combination of the two. Several pharmacological groups of antidepressants are available; prescription of medication and any subsequent changes should be carefully monitored by either a GP or mental health specialist. However, it is important to realize that if one type of medication does not seem to be helpful, this should be discussed with the prescribing specialist as alternatives are available.

Two main types of talking therapies or psychotherapies are effective in treating depression. Cognitive behavioural therapy (CBT) helps people with depression to restructure negative thought patterns, and interpersonal therapy (IPT) helps people understand and work through troubled relationships at the root of their depression

Anxiety

As with depression, anxiety is something which is part of the human condition. It has a useful biological function, as a reaction to personal danger and threat. This reaction prepares us to face the danger with 'fight or flight' and is a multi-system response incorporating a person's history and memory, the social situation and automatic biochemical changes in the body.

Anxiety can be a helpful response for us. Low levels of mild anxiety and the resulting increase in arousal help us cope in difficult situations, but only up to a point. Feeling anxious is a normal phenomenon, usually occurring when faced with an identifiable fear, danger or threat.

In anxiety disorders, the anxious response is prompted by triggers which are harder to pin down. The level of anxiety is experienced as excessive and debilitating and is longer lasting. The symptoms of anxiety fall into four categories:

1. *cognitive*: fear and worry about what might happen, thoughts racing or going blank, memory and concentration difficulties, difficulty with decision making

2. *emotional*: excessive fear, irritability, feeling confused, impatience and being easily angered

3. *somatic or physical*: dry mouth, tightness or pain in the chest, shaking and trembling, sweating, palpitations, flushing and blushing, nausea, vomiting, diarrhoea, muscle pains, poor sleep

4. *behavioural*: avoidance of situations or people, a heightened startle response, using alcohol or drugs in order to cope.

There are several types of anxiety disorder which may be diagnosed. The main disorders can be summarized as follows:

-   *Generalized anxiety disorder (GAD)* is excessive anxiety which has no fixed focus. Sometimes thought of as 'worry about worry', mild sufferers may be able to function relatively normally, but profound GAD will have a significant impact on everyday life.

-   *Social anxiety disorder* is a strong fear of social situations and of being judged negatively by others. People with severe social phobia habitually feel stupid, unlikeable, dirty or ashamed of themselves. The resulting avoidance of social situations leads to a sense of being alone, left out and worthless.

-   *Post-traumatic stress disorder (PTSD)* is associated with witnessing or experiencing a traumatic event. This is dealt with in more detail in the next section.

-   *Obsessive-compulsive disorder (OCD)* can be considered as a type of anxiety disorder. People with OCD experience obsessions and/or compulsions. Obsessions may be thoughts, pictures or impulses which appear in the mind repeatedly and intrusively, such as thoughts of contamination or about hurting someone. Compulsions are rituals which must be performed repeatedly, such as checking that a door is locked, or repeating a phrase to ensure that negative events do not happen. Compulsions may temporarily reduce the distress and anxiety caused by obsessive thinking, but this is only short-lived as performing the compulsions themselves increases anxiety and distress.

-   *Specific phobias* are a marked fear or anxiety about a partcular situation, object or event. The fear evoked is intense, consistent and may be linked with panic attacks. Although many people will say, 'I have a phobia about such and such…' they are usually describing the normal, short-lived fears most members of the population experience from time to time. Specific phobias are qualitatively different and much more debilitating and intense. Multiple specific phobias are common; three-quarters of the people diagnosed with specific phobia fear more than one situation, object or event.

- *Panic disorder* refers to experiencing unexpected, unpredictable and repeated panic attacks. Panic attacks are spontaneous feelings of anxiety, terror or impending doom which quickly rise to a peak. Physical symptoms include heart palpitations, chest pain and shortness of breath. Although people with any anxiety disorder may have panic attacks, in panic disorder these have no obvious trigger.

Anxiety and learning disability

Anxiety disorders are thought to be reported at least as often, if not more, in the population of people with learning disabilities when compared with the general population. However, they are still considered likely to be under-reported and under-diagnosed (Joop and Keys, 2001). In the general population, anxiety disorder often occurs in conjunction with other mental health problems, particularly depression. It may be more difficult to distinguish between the two when a person has learning disabilities, as diagnosis depends on the finer detail of a person's description. With respect to symptoms of anxiety, a picture of the observable symptoms (e.g. avoidance, shaking, nausea, irritability) from a friend, partner or close professional can go some way to aiding diagnosis. This is particularly helpful when the person experiencing the anxiety is unable to give a clear description of their internal thoughts and feelings. Hurley (2008) suggests that fearfulness and withdrawal accompanied by low mood and crying are particularly likely to be seen in people with a learning disability with anxiety difficulties as opposed to depression or another mental health problem.

What are the implications for parents with anxiety disorder and learning disabilities?

Parents with learning disabilities suffering from high levels of anxiety will share the same range of difficulties identified in the general population, but the overall picture will be more complex as these difficulties will also interact with their learning disability.

The physical symptoms of anxiety affect everyday life and routines, interfering with appetite, sleep and concentration, and so the ability to cope with everyday stresses and strains is reduced. Chronic worry interferes with cognitive processing and will impede or slow down problem solving and the ability to manage the unexpected. Long-term anxiety and emotional stress can trigger a number of health problems associated with the constant triggering of the 'fight or flight' system in the body, for example digestive problems, loss of libido and lowered immunity to common illnesses such as coughs and colds. All of this takes its toll on the individual's ability to cope with the demands of being a parent and on her management of relationships with a partner, extended family and professionals. People who worry excessively may try to self-medicate, developing harmful lifestyle habits such as overeating, smoking cigarettes or using alcohol and non-prescribed drugs.

Treatment options

In cases of mild anxiety, self-help in the form of lifestyle changes may be sufficient, Exercise, eating a healthy balanced diet, talking over problems with friends and increasing opportunities for relaxation in daily routines are all recommended. Community-based relaxation or exercise groups may also be helpful.

In more severe cases, the treatment likely to be offered via the GP will vary with diagnosis. Ideally, talking treatments should be recommended before prescribing medication (NICE, 2011).

Talking treatments (counselling or therapy) aim to help the individual explore and resolve problems which contribute to raised anxiety. The development of a range of strategies to manage anxiety is an important part of this process.

The most commonly prescribed talking treatment for anxiety is CBT, because there is reliable evidence that it can be effective. CBT in anxiety focusses on recognizing core patterns of thinking, working out ways of changing these patterns and enabling the individual to move on with their lives. Diaries, charts and pictorial aids may be used to help people with learning disabilities understand and remember work undertaken during therapy, together with simplified structure and an extended number of shorter sessions (Morgan, 2009).

Applied relaxation therapy is often recommended as a treatment for anxiety. It involves learning how to relax your muscles, initially in a non-threatening situation and then in situations which are likely to provoke anxiety. It is usually delivered by a trained therapist in (often) weekly sessions for a period of several months. Mindfulness meditation therapy is an alternative way of relaxing and refocussing. These relaxation-based therapies are often recommended for GAD.

As part of a treatment regime, medication may be prescribed. There are different types of medication which can be helpful in managing anxiety. Some primarily affect the physical symptoms; others are more effective at helping people feel calmer. Sometimes medication is helpful in controlling overt symptoms of anxiety, thus allowing the individual to participate effectively in talking treatment.

Post-traumatic stress disorder (PTSD)

As part of daily life, we can all experience or find ourselves in frightening, threatening and uncontrollable situations. Many people manage to come to terms with such experiences over time without needing professional help, but sometimes the traumatic experience triggers the long-term and debilitating reaction called PTSD.

People who have experienced repeated severe neglect, abuse or violence can have a similar set of reactions. Some clinicians refer to this as Complex PTSD.

Symptoms of PTSD

Symptoms of PTSD vary from person to person, but these usually fall within three categories:

1. *Flashbacks and nightmares*: the person relives the event over and over in realistic detail. This can happen during sleep as nightmares, or unexpectedly burst into daytime thoughts as flashbacks.

2. *Avoidance and numbing*: in order to avoid thinking about the traumatic experience, people may try to distract themselves by avoiding (or trying to avoid) anything that reminds them of the event. Alternatively, they may keep very busy working or becoming absorbed in distracting activities. Sometimes a way of avoiding the pain of traumatic memories is by trying not to feel anything at all, communicating less and dulling down emotional reactions.

3. *Hypervigilance and over-alertness*: the person feels the need to be alert and on the lookout for possible danger all the time. Under these circumstances relaxation is impossible, levels of anxiety are high and sleep is disturbed. Hypervigilant people appear jumpy and irritable much of the time.

PTSD and learning disability

Research into this topic indicates that people with a learning disability are particularly vulnerable to the development of PTSD for a number of reasons:

- People with a learning disability are more likely to have experienced traumatic events, particularly physical and sexual abuse (Focht-New *et al.*, 2008).

- The range of experiences which could be regarded as traumatic is greater in people with learning disabilities (Martorell and Tsakanikos, 2008).

- The cumulative experience of continued failure and negative life experiences increases vulnerability (Mevissen and de Jongh, 2010).

- Realizing that you are different from the rest of the population and subject to stigmatizing labelling is intrinsically traumatizing (Levitas and Gilson, 2001).

- Lower developmental levels correlate with higher risk of PTSD development and more serious symptoms (Breslau, Lucia and Alvarado, 2006).

- Early separation from parents through institutionalization combined with limited experience of resolving negative life events further increases vulnerability (Tomasulo and Razza, 2007).

Despite these factors, prevalence rates, assessment and treatment of PTSD in people with learning disabilities is not well understood. Although the presentation of people with mild learning disabilities is considered to be much the same as in the rest of the population, the confounding features associated with learning disability complicate the overall picture and may even serve to obscure trauma symptoms.

What are the implications for parents with PTSD and learning disabilities?

Parents who are having difficulty caring for their children may well have a history of trauma themselves. Early experience of trauma disrupts biological and psychological maturation processes and is associated with the development of emotional and behavioural difficulties (van der Kolk, 1996). When the parent has a learning disability, vulnerability to disruption of these processes increases.

In particular, parents with a learning disability may:

- have difficulty identifying events as traumatic

- be unable to describe their experiences clearly

- be supported by people who may dismiss potentially traumatizing events

- be supported by people who have no knowledge of their history

- be supported by people who have low recognition of the cumulative effect of negative life events.

This leaves parents open to coping with the intense fear and hopelessness of PTSD virtually alone. Additional mental health problems are often linked with PTSD, especially depression, agoraphobia and social phobia. Sometimes behaviour that appears to be related to a learning disability may be either caused or made worse by traumatic experience. Behaviour such as impulsive acting out rather than being able to think through a reaction to distress, finding it hard to discuss emotion, having difficulty linking events causally, problems monitoring personal behaviour (and the consequences) and poor self-concept may be written off as part of an individual's learning disability rather than noted, explored and understood with sensitivity.

You may be able to access historical information which can be important in the identification of trauma experience; this may be available from a range of sources including family, friends and more formal records. Simply listening carefully to the parent's own account of their life and experiences supports identification of distress from which a joint understanding of trauma (between the listener and the parent) can be constructed.

Treatment options

SELF-HELP

Reviewing routine and lifestyle can be a powerful way of managing symptoms of PTSD, but of course this will depend on each person's own resources. PTSD symptoms can be helped by supporting the individual to:

- keep life as normal as possible with an everyday routine of working, eating and exercising

- talk about what happened to someone who will listen carefully and respect their confidence

- take extra care of themselves as their concentration may not be as good as usual

- try different ways of relaxing: exercises, listening to music, yoga

- go back to where the traumatic event happened, if the person feels this will be helpful (not everyone does), but support for this should be carefully planned

- avoid drinking more coffee and alcohol or smoking more

- talk about what has happened and seek treatment if needed.

TALKING TREATMENTS (PSYCHOTHERAPY)

The forms of talking treatments that have been shown to be the most effective focus on recall of the traumatic experience. This helps the individual make sense of what has happened to her and recall it in a controlled way (i.e. without being overtaken by distress) in order to process the associated memories, store those memories in a less emotive manner and begin to move on to new topics and activities.

EYE MOVEMENT DESENSITIZATION AND REPROCESSING (EMDR)

This is a fairly recently developed technique which uses rhythmic eye movements to help the brain to process flashbacks and to decrease the emotional power and make sense of the traumatic experience. It may sound odd, but it has been shown to work in the general population and a small number of case studies report positive effects when used with people with a learning disability.

GROUP THERAPY

This involves meeting with a group of other people who have been through the same, or a similar, traumatic event. It can be easier to talk about what happened if you are with other people who have been through a similar experience.

MEDICATION

Antidepressant medication can be prescribed to help manage the severity of symptoms and relieve depression. Sometimes short-term anxiety-reducing medication may also be prescribed to aid poor sleep and reduce levels of anxiety.

BODY-FOCUSSED THERAPIES

These treatments aim to help the individual cope with feelings of stress, distress and hyperarousal – that sense of being 'on guard' most of the time – by teaching or promoting relaxation and stress management. Relaxation therapy and mindfulness meditation therapy are all used in this context as well as complementary therapies such as massage, acupuncture, reflexology, yoga and tai chi.

Attention deficit hyperactivity disorder (ADHD)

For many years, professionals reassured parents whose children were diagnosed with ADHD that they would 'grow out of it' by late adolescence. Over the last 20 years, this belief has been tested, as clinical reports of the condition lasting into adulthood became more numerous. More recently still, outcome studies suggest that some 60% of adults with a childhood diagnosis of ADHD continue to demonstrate symptoms of ADHD; of those 60%, about one-third will go on to develop significant problems related to the continuity and severity of their symptoms of ADHD.

What is ADHD?

ADHD was originally thought of as a disorder occurring in childhood. The core symptoms of hyperactivity, impulsivity and inattention are well known and recognized.

A strong genetic component is evident in ADHD; the risk of a parent with ADHD having a child with the disorder is 57% (Biederman *et al.*, 1998). Risk factors are both psychosocial (e.g. neglect, poor parental care and management, family breakdown) and physical (e.g. prematurity, birth complications, maternal tobacco and alcohol consumption during pregnancy), with a contribution from neurobiological factors such as closed head trauma.

Prevalence studies of sex distribution in ADHD produce results varying from 1.5:1 to 2:1 (males:females) (Heptinstall and Taylor, 2002), but it is suggested that girls may be under-represented because of diagnostic bias. In any event, the sex ratio seems to even out with age. In general, females with ADHD seem to experience more anxiety, mood instability and interpersonal difficulties, where as males are more likely to present with violence, aggression and antisocial behaviour problems.

ADHD and learning disabilities

People both with and without a learning disability experience ADHD, although some clinicians have suggested that the disorder is more prevalent in people with mild learning disabilities. The general consensus is that many of the features of ADHD are seen in people with a learning disability at a milder level; the ADHD serves to emphasize these qualities and complicate the clinical picture. The symptoms of ADHD, therefore, are the same as is seen in the general population, but are likely to be emphasized because of the existing learning disability.

How does ADHD present in adults?

It is agreed that simply applying childhood symptoms to adults does not give an accurate clinical picture. The core features of hyperactivity, impulsivity and inattention have a different presentation in adults with a less overt manifestation. Symptoms associated with adult ADHD are:

- poor organizational skills
- impulsivity, seen in impatience and high irritability
- restlessness
- mood fluctuation
- forgetfulness
- poor focus
- risk taking
- carelessness and a lack of attention to detail
- poor social timing, interrupting, poorly thought-out responses.

What are the implications for parents with ADHD?

The effect of having ADHD on parenting skills will, of course, vary with the severity of the condition. They can be grouped under the following headings:

- *Attention*: this applies to focussing on a task, and shifting the focus of attention as necessary. The individual struggles to engage in tasks which are long, boring, repetitive or tedious – such as basic housework, meal preparation and some indirect aspects of child care. It is important to identify tasks that are likely to be a problem and maximize attention by reducing distraction and setting small goals.

- *Memory problems*: remembering shopping, appointments and even to feed your child are some of the memory tasks involved in parenting. A range of aids can be developed to help, but the parent must be motivated to use these in order for them to work.

- *Organization*: chaotic organizational skills are likely to become more marked in adult life. Household organization, from getting the washing done to knowing where your child is playing, is part of safe parenting and can be a major challenge for a parent who never finishes one task completely and flits between tasks ineffectively. Poor time management skills are associated with organizational difficulties and will interfere with everyday life. Routines and methodical structure can help with the regulation of these difficulties.

- *Impulsivity*: this is likely to be linked to low tolerance of frustration and is seen in the apparent inability to delay gratification or consider the consequences of actions first. At best, this may present some risks to the child in an impulsive parents' care; at worst, where there is poor impulse control leading to aggression, there may be significant risks to others.

- *Mood*: frustration, anger, anxiety, low mood and mood fluctuation are commonly experienced mood variations in ADHD; all are likely to interfere with the parenting process and make the parent seem unpredictable to the child. Depending on the intensity of the difficulties, environmental changes, goal setting or medical treatment may all be options to be considered.

Diagnosis and treatment options

Diagnosis will be the province of an appropriately qualified psychiatrist or clinical psychologist. An indication of whether a diagnosis should be sought is found in the answer to these questions:

- Did the parent have a firm diagnosis of ADHD as a child?

- If this was so, are the symptoms still evident in her everyday life?

As in the management of childhood ADHD, stimulant medication may be prescribed in order to control the core symptoms. The effectiveness of this medication varies from individual to individual; any prescription will be closely monitored by the specialist involved. Where appropriate, pharmacological treatment of low mood and anxiety can be effective, but this depends on individual presentation.

In adult ADHD, it is not only the core symptoms that require treatment, but also the cumulative effect of a lifetime of having ADHD: psychosocial problems, skill deficits and additional mental health symptoms. It is recognized that talking treatments require some adaptation in order to be helpful for people who have particular cognitive difficulties, high intolerance and a low boredom threshold. Techniques such as using a variety of presentation modes, frequent breaks, using exercises to maintain attention and building in immediate and longer-term rewards may be incorporated in a general approach which uses a combination of the following:

- *Psychoeducation*: providing information about ADHD and providing an opportunity to consider the meaning and impact of the diagnosis on the individual.

- *Motivational interviewing*: these techniques are designed to be client-centred and actively promote change at the same time as developing a positive belief that change will happen.

- *CBT*: this focusses on reframing and restructuring the past, and, through a structured programme, developing and practising behaviours that help the individual attain her goals.

Where the parent has a learning disability in addition to a diagnosis of ADHD, adaptations must be carefully balanced in order to promote accessibility as well as treatment efficacy.

A very few areas have a specialized adult ADHD service, usually attached to the mental health services. These services are able to offer specifically adapted programmes of support and facilitate self-help and support groups for their clients.

Eating disorders

Eating disorders (some service user groups prefer the term *eating distress*) are described as severe disturbances in eating behaviour. Common signs that someone may be developing a problematic relationship with eating and food are:

- seeming preoccupied with body shape or weight
- fixating on calories, food or nutrition
- always being on a diet, even when thin
- rapid, unexplained weight loss or weight gain
- taking laxatives or diet pills
- exercising compulsively
- making excuses to get out of eating
- avoiding social situations that involve food
- going to the bathroom right after meals
- eating alone, at night or in secret
- hoarding high-calorie food.

There are a number of sub-diagnoses, which depend on the particular presenting symptoms:

- *anorexia nervosa*, where the person is intensely afraid of gaining weight, will not maintain a healthy body weight and has a disturbed perception of her size and shape
- *bulimia nervosa*, the central features of this disorder being episodes of binge eating followed by behaviour designed to limit weight gain, such as forced vomiting or laxative use
- *binge eating disorder*, where the person feels repeatedly compelled to binge eat, sometimes followed by an attempt to compensate with periods of undereating; binges may be pre-planned and involve 'special' foods
- *eating disorder (not otherwise specified)*, where the diagnosis covers other disorders of eating which do not meet the specific criteria to warrant one of the above diagnoses.

Eating disorders and learning disability

It seems likely that classic eating disorders are very much under-diagnosed in the learning disabled population (Hove, 2004). The reason for this is that unless the person has only a very mild learning disability, and relatively good verbal skills, assessment of some of the key diagnostic components – such as assessing perception of body image – lacks clarity and accuracy, even if observers are available to give objective supporting evidence.

Research evidence focusses on reports of single or small group case reports, with many of these providing descriptive information only. Little is known about risk factors for the development of eating disorders in learning disability.

Summarizing research in the area, Poindexter and Loschen (2007) conclude that standard diagnostic criteria can be successfully applied to people with moderate and mild learning disability if they are able to communicate about self-image. If this is not possible, then pictorial prompts together with information from observers may be used as a diagnostic aid.

What are the implications for parents with an eating disorder and learning disabilities?

The risks to the physical health of mothers with a learning disability and eating disorder will be the same as those observed in the general population. Pregnancy, with its intrinsic changes in body shape and size, can act as a trigger to women who have recovered from an eating disorder, although, conversely, some report less worry about eating and food at this time. An eating disorder will stress the body and results in a higher level of pregnancy complications, potentially affecting the health of both the mother and baby in the short and longer term. Depending on the intensity of health problems, this may have a significant effect on the child's needs and the parent's coping abilities.

Eating disorders have been shown to have psychological consequences for the person with a learning disability. Malnutrition affects attention, memory and cognitive processing and is likely to be associated with lowered mood (Trotter, 1997). In the general population, eating disorders are associated with a wide range of physical, psychological and behavioural effects. A link between eating disorders and alcohol and drug use has been identified (Behar, 2004). Symptoms of stress, low self-esteem and affective disorders (Gravestock, 2008) and a high prevalence of self-injury and attempted suicide in people with eating disorders have been well established (Kostro, Lerman and Attia, 2014). Although these areas have not been specifically researched in the field of learning disability, it is reasonable to expect that similar effects will be evident in at least people with mild and moderate learning disabilities. Assessment for suicide risk should be routinely included for people with learning disabilities who have an eating disorder as part of any planning or treatment.

Treatment options

Simple steps such as talking to supportive friends and family members, and trying to change negative routines with respect to food can be helpful early steps. Breaking free from a negative relationship with food can be extremely difficult and others around the person may not always be understanding.

Seeking help early on from people who are experienced in treating eating problems is important.

More formal treatment is often multi-professional, with input from medical staff, dieticians, talking therapy and possibly medication. Medical care and monitoring are essential to ensure that long-term effects of any eating disorder are minimized. Dieticians will advise on healthy eating, ensuring that the correct balance of nutrients is achieved, and oversee a healthy weight gain. When the person with eating disorders has a learning disability, an adapted psychoeducational approach is helpful to promote understanding and new learning (Vanstraelen, Holt and Bouras, 2003).

Common talking therapies for eating problems include:

- CBT

- IPT, which looks at the connection between relationships in the individual's life and the emotions that are associated with these relationships

- dialectical behaviour therapy (DBT), which explores emotions and the part these play in our lives; at the same time acceptance of the self is encouraged as a specific aim

- group and family therapies.

Guidelines on the treatment of eating disorders recommend talking treatments as a first choice. There are no drugs that treat eating disorders specifically, but underlying causes of the problems (such as depression or other mental health problems) may be identified and treated with appropriate medication.

In cases where the eating disorder is very serious, if other kinds of treatment haven't worked, or if the home environment is compounding the problem, admission to hospital or a specialized clinic may be considered.

Psychosis and schizophrenia

Psychotic 'episodes' as they are called may have a number of causes. Although it is relatively unusual, major stressful events (such as losing a close friend) can prompt an episode; it can also be the result of a physical illness (e.g. a severe infection) or the use of illegal drugs (e.g. cannabis). Schizophrenia is a type of psychosis; in order to be diagnosed with schizophrenia, an individual must have experienced more than one psychotic episode, along with other symptoms, within a six-month period.

In psychosis and schizophrenia, we see a broad range of very unusual behaviours which friends and relatives of the person affected find very difficult to understand. These unusual behaviours are highly disruptive to the lives of both the person experiencing the symptoms and the family members and friends who are trying to cope with the effects of this mental illness.

This group of disorders is defined by a number of key features:

- *Delusions*: fixed beliefs not open to change even if evidence to the contrary is presented.

- *Hallucinations*: vivid sensory experiences which occur without any external trigger. Auditory hallucinations (e.g. hearing voices) are the most common type of sensory experience.

- *Disorganized thinking (thought disorder)*: this has a significant effect on communication. The person may flit from one idea to another, answer questions by referring to related or unrelated topics, or, at times, appear generally incomprehensible.

- *Abnormal motor behaviour*: this may show some variation, ranging from childish silly behaviour or unpredictable agitation to catatonic behaviour where verbal and motor behaviour becomes severely limited. Stereotyped or odd routine movements such as staring or echoing speech may also be evident.

- *Negative symptoms*, such as a lack of emotional expression, low motivation to carry out everyday activities and a decrease in the experience of pleasure.

The person with a psychotic disorder is likely to experience some rather than all of these features. Symptoms may be evident over the short term (as in brief psychotic disorder) or longer term (as in schizophrenia). The risk of depression and suicide in people with psychosis is high.

Postpartum (puerperal) psychosis

This is a serious mental health disorder which affects about 1 in every 1000 new mothers. It often develops very suddenly, usually within days or weeks of giving birth, and requires immediate attention.

Women are at risk of developing postpartum psychosis if they have a family or personal history of severe mental illness, particularly bipolar disorder and schizophrenia. The symptoms usually respond well to treatment (which may include admission to a specialized mother and baby unit). Most mothers recover within a few weeks, although sometimes the recovery period is much longer.

Psychosis, schizophrenia and learning disability

The research literature recognizes an increased occurrence of psychotic disorders in the population of people with a learning disability. However, diagnosis and recognition of psychosis (hallucinations, delusions or paranoia) remains an area of particular difficulty. In the general population, diagnosis is based on an interview with the individual and an evaluation of her description of internal perceptual experiences. This method may be successfully used with a person who has a mild learning disability but relatively good verbal skills; however, simple and naïve descriptions may be dismissed and compliant individuals can be talked out of their beliefs by those in authority (Royal College of Psychiatrists, 2001).

Observation of the individual and corroborative reports from those who know the person well are helpful, but the information gained must be interpreted carefully. For example, a person experiencing sensory experiences associated with a migraine headache may well appear to be looking at something that isn't there; but if we know that this person often has migraine headaches, it gives a likely explanation.

More specifically, people with mild learning disabilities have been shown to be more likely to experience hallucinations (particularly auditory hallucinations) without delusion and tend to present more symptoms involving actions rather than thoughts (Favrod *et al.*, 2007).

What are the implications for parents with psychosis and schizophrenia?

Psychosis is defined as a major mental illness and as such has a significant impact on the life of the individual and her family. In psychosis, a person's ability to think clearly, make sound judgements, respond emotionally, communicate, stay in touch with reality and behave appropriately are all impaired. Thought processes are affected so that the person has difficulty understanding and evaluating what is happening, even in quite ordinary situations. This affects the person's ability to manage everyday life, and will have a significant impact on her parenting behaviour. Miller and Finnerty (1996) found that, in a sample of mothers in treatment for schizophrenia and related disorders, over half lost custody of their children at some point in the child's life. As a co-occurring learning disability will magnify difficulties with thoughts and behaviour, it seems reasonable to conclude that the risk of serious problems in their life as a parent is high, particularly in the absence of strong support networks.

Treatment options

Most psychotic illnesses can be effectively treated with medication combined with psychotherapy. Antipsychotic medications offer effective control of the most intrusive symptoms, such as delusions, hallucinations and thinking problems. Anti-anxiety and antidepressant medication may also be offered, depending on the course of each person's illness.

Every person being treated for a psychotic disorder will respond and recover at her own pace, some recovering quickly and others needing to continue treatment for much longer. Sometimes a short stay in hospital may be needed whilst symptoms are stabilized. Many people who have a diagnosis of schizophrenia do not experience a complete remission of symptoms. The aim is to manage symptoms, with a combination of psychosocial therapies, medications and individual support.

Psychotherapy, or talking therapy, used in conjunction with medication, can help with adjustment, supporting the family unit (family education/therapy) and helping develop techniques to manage intrusive thoughts, voices and apathy (CBT). Rehabilitative approaches help people understand their disorder, particularly the signs that signal potential relapse and equip individuals with life and social skills to aid the process of readjustment. Various kinds of group support may be available from skills-based (e.g. social skills groups) to self-help groups, facilitated by people using the service, aimed at sharing problems and experiences.

Personality disorders

The idea of personality in mental health refers to the individual characteristics or personality traits which develop throughout childhood and early adulthood. Usually, by their early twenties people have developed their own ways of thinking, feeling and behaving: in other words, their individual personality. Our personality allows us to fit in with our cultural background and social networks and to get on with our lives. Some people find that elements of their personality make this process of moving forward in life and getting on with others problematic. These elements are difficult to change and, because of this, go on making life difficult. When personality traits are unchanging, severely unhelpful to the individual and cause that person distress, a diagnosis of personality disorder may be considered.

Personality disorders are categorized into three groups, each with shared overall characteristics:

- *Cluster A*: with suspicious or eccentric characteristics

- *Cluster B*: showing emotional, dramatic and impulsive thoughts and behaviour

- *Cluster C*: showing anxious and fearful traits.

But a person can have the characteristics of more than one personality disorder and will not necessarily fit tidily into one clear definition.

The following gives more detail about the individual disorders within clusters:

Cluster A

- People with *paranoid* personality disorder are likely to be easily rejected, suspicious and mistrustful.

- People with *schizoid* personality disorder may appear cold and detached, yet have a rich fantasy world.

- People with *schizotypal* personality disorder are eccentric and unusual; they have difficulties with thinking and can have delusional thoughts.

Cluster B

- People with *antisocial* or dissocial personality disorders show little guilt, concern or remorse about their actions. They may find it difficult to control frustration and anger and are unlikely to learn from experience.

- People with *borderline* or emotionally unstable personality disorders enter into intense and unstable relationships, finding it hard to control their emotions. Episodes of self-harm or suicidal thinking are likely.

- People with *histrionic* personality disorder are self-centered, dramatic and highly suggestible. They can be apparently highly emotional or seductive but with little real depth.

- People with *narcissistic* personality disorder crave attention and success, yet show little empathy for others.

Cluster C

- People with *obsessive-compulsive* personality disorder are cautious, rigid and worry in their search for perfection. They focus on order as a way to control messy areas of life. They may have obsessional thoughts and concerns, but these are not as severe as in obsessive-compulsive disorder.

- People with *avoidant* personality disorder tend to be very anxious and tense, needing to be liked and accepted, yet having strong feelings of insecurity and inferiority.

- People with *dependent* personality disorder will try to rely on others to make decisions and help them cope. They can seem clingy and are likely to feel easily abandoned.

As well as the personality disorder itself, the tendency for life to be more difficult for people with a personality disorder is likely to trigger additional mental health problems such as depression. Difficulties caused by self-medicating with drugs and alcohol are also associated with this group of disorders. Personality disorders are not usually diagnosed until early adulthood and research evidence suggests that personality disorders tend to improve slowly with age.

Some mental health specialists disagree with the use of the term *personality disorder*, maintaining that it is unnecessarily stigmatizing and does not help with deciding programmes of treatment. Rather than trying to attach unhelpful labels to individuals, they prefer to focus on the needs of the person and the supports that will help her to manage everyday life more effectively.

Personality disorders and learning disability

The utility of a diagnosis of personality disorder is similarly debated by clinicians working in the field of learning disability. As in the diagnosis of other mental health disorders, good verbal communication skills are required in order to describe internal thoughts and beliefs; these may be limited in people with a learning disability, making accurate diagnosis difficult. In addition, some of the diagnostic criteria for personality disorder can appear to overlap with features of learning disability, such as delayed maturity and social adjustment difficulties. This leads to confusion if the developmental stage of the individual is not carefully considered. Autistic traits also overlap significantly with features of schizoid and schizotypal personality disorders, adding further potential confusion. General recommendations for the diagnosis of personality disorders in learning disabilities advise the following:

- Differences in the development of personality characteristics in people with a learning disability, when compared with the general population, should be considered and a higher age threshold (at least over 21) for diagnosis should be used (Royal College of Psychiatrists, 2001).

- The initial diagnosis should be unspecified personality disorder. The need for further sub-classification can then be carefully considered.

- It is more difficult to apply the sub-classifications of dissocial, paranoid (Goldberg *et al.*, 1995) and dependent and avoidant personality disorder to this group (Alexander and Cooray, 2003).

What are the implications for parents with a personality disorder and learning disabilities?

A diagnosis of personality disorder is indicative of serious mental illness. Presentation will be different for each individual, but the effects of the personality disorder will interact with and intensify any learning disability. Possible effects are:

- difficulties with clarity of thinking, understanding what is expected, making decisions

- managing impulsivity, both behavioural and in decision making

- disruption of much needed support networks

- mis-attribution of the motivations of others leading to difficulty engaging with support/professionals

- inconsistent emotional presentation

- difficulties with practical and emotional priorities

- a lack of predictability leading to disruption of the attachment relationship between the parent and child.

Treatment options

Treatment for people with personality disorders can be psychological (talking therapies) and/or physical (medication), although support and self-help are important in helping people with personality disorders manage their lives.

TALKING TREATMENTS

A number of psychotherapies have been seen to work within the general population. Of these few have been explored for use with people with learning disabilities and personality disorder, although single case studies are beginning to be reported in the literature. CBT is perhaps the best-known approach, but dialectical behaviour therapy and cognitive analytic therapy are beginning to be explored with this group.

MEDICATION

Medication cannot cure a personality disorder; the prescription of medication in personality disorders is not advised by the National Institute for Care and Health Excellence. However, some clinicians prescribe medications in order to alleviate symptoms. Low-dose antipsychotic medication can help with paranoid thoughts, antidepressants can help with mood and emotional difficulties, and mood stabilizers can help with impulsivity and mood instability.

Support and self-help

A generally healthy lifestyle will help people with personality disorders manage their lives effectively. People with learning disabilities may need additional support and encouragement to incorporate as many of these ideas as possible into their lives:

- good sleep, eating and daily routines

- eating a healthy diet

- incorporating relaxing elements into the day, such as taking a bath or listening to music

- avoiding drinking too much alcohol or using street drugs

- taking simple but regular exercise; simply taking a walk is helpful

- taking up an interest or hobby

- staying positively occupied during the day; part-time or voluntary working could be considered, or involvement in a community group

- having someone to talk to; this could be a friend, relative, therapist or counsellor.

It is important to help the person with practical tasks so she doesn't become overwhelmed – sorting bills out or arranging things, talking to officials and so on.

Summary

The main points of this chapter can be summarized as follows:

- It is now clearly recognized that not only do people with learning disabilities experience the same range of mental health disorders as everybody else but they are particularly vulnerable to the development of mental health disorders.

- Given this recognition, it is a concern that mental health problems in this population are not well recognized and likely to be under-diagnosed.

- Problems observed may be explained as part of the learning disability itself (diagnostic overshadowing) or hidden by the appearance of coping well.

- Diagnosis is often reliant on the person's self-report of internal thoughts and emotions; even if the individual's communication skills are relatively good, corroborative information from other sources is helpful.

- Diagnostic criteria developed for the general population may, with care and some adaptation, be applied to people with mild learning disabilities.

- However, the complexities of gaining an accurate understanding of a person's behaviour in the context of a learning disability should not be underestimated.

Chapter 5

Autism Spectrum Disorder

In this chapter we look at the autism spectrum and autism spectrum disorders (ASD), including Asperger syndrome (AS) and higher-functioning autism (HFA) as follows:

- a general description of the spectrum

- clarification of the different terms and labels used around ASD

- how ASD affects the individual, describing symptoms, development and inheritance

- parents with ASD

- some suggestions of how best to work with parents who have ASD.

What is ASD?

ASD is a developmental condition which begins to be recognized early in life and continues to be evident throughout the life of that individual. It is called a spectrum disorder because there is a wide range of symptoms and a range of intensity. There will be differences in how the ASD presents, depending on the severity of symptoms, chronological age and developmental level of each person. ASD occurs across the range of cognitive abilities; some people have accompanying learning disability (about 50% of people with ASD have a learning disability; NICE, 2012) whereas others have average or above-average intelligence. However, each person on the spectrum shares common problems with social behaviour, empathy, flexibility and communication even though there is tremendous variation from person to person.

ASD is often described in terms of the 'Triad of Impairments', which describe the core set of difficulties:

- *Difficulties with social interactions*: people with ASD find it difficult to understand others' emotions and point of view; hence their response may be unexpected, confusing or appear self-centred. They may seem aloof and uninterested in social approaches.

- *Difficulties with verbal and non-verbal communication*: people with ASD have difficulty understanding the nuances and subtlety of both verbal and non-verbal language. Communication may present a real problem leading to misunderstandings and even social isolation.

- *Difficulties with imagination*: people with ASD find it difficult to predict what might happen and think through the social ramifications of a given situation, giving rise to mistakes, misunderstandings and potential crises. They are more likely to concentrate on detail, even trivia, rather than the whole picture.

These difficulties are often accompanied by:

- *Repetitive behaviour*: people with ASD might repeat certain words or activities, or get 'stuck' on a subject or idea. Their life may be governed by routines which are not open to change.

- *Sensory sensitivities*: these are significant sensitivities to anything from a wide range of sight, sound, touch and motion, and can be highly debilitating.

These key features will be evident in an individual's developmental history, although some difficulties may be masked by compensation or supports. For example, a child with ASD who has a supportive sibling close in age may learn to mimic social behaviour without developing more generalized social understanding. He then learns how to manage certain situations, but because he lacks the generalized understanding, he does not cope well with unusual or very different situations. The triad is not the whole story, as inherited family traits and individual personalities will add to the overall picture of each person with ASD. This will also vary with age as people learn to adapt to their circumstances and develop strategies for managing their life and ASD.

Labelling

There are a number of labels attached to the ASD spectrum, which can be confusing. Of course, the idea of labelling is considered by some to be less than helpful, even pejorative, but the labels are explained here so that you will be able to recognize and understand the names in use.

The label ASD covers the whole autism spectrum – everybody who has recognized autistic traits. It is a 'spectrum' because different people with ASD will have different presentations, as explained earlier. In the most recent edition (2013) of the Diagnostic and Statistical Manual of Mental Disorders (DSM-5, see Chapter 1) ASD is used as a single overarching diagnostic term and the use of sub-types is not encouraged. Instead DSM-5 suggests classification of severity of symptoms into three categories which refer to the amount of support required. They are:

1. *Requiring very substantial support.* People in this category will have severe communication deficits and highly inflexible behaviour.

2. *Requiring substantial support.* In this category people will have marked communication deficits, limited social behaviour and difficulty coping with change.

3. *Requiring support.* People in this category will have noticeable impairments in social communication, decreased social behaviour and some inflexibility.

However, historically some specific sub-diagnoses have been and continue to be commonly used and descriptions of these follow, bearing in mind that all these come under the umbrella of ASD.

People with AS and HFA have the difficulties with social communication, social interaction and social imagination – that is, the triad of impairments seen in all people with ASD. However, AS and HFA are usually accompanied by at least average, high average or superior levels of intelligence. Sometimes the person has an unusual and outstanding ability or skill – often one that requires either innate talent or particular attention to detail, such as working with computers, complex mathematical calculations or artistic or musical ability. Some clinicians working in the field consider that the distinction made between AS and HFA as separate conditions is artificial. However, the main difference recognized is that in AS we expect fewer language problems and no history of language delay. In HFA, a developmental history of language difficulty or delay is present, which may linger into adulthood.

The term *atypical autism* may be used to describe an unusual presentation or combination of symptoms; these would feature the triad of impairments, but perhaps be particularly skewed to one or other of the diagnostic criteria – in other words, not the usual picture.

The complicated (and rather unhelpful) label Pervasive Developmental Disorder Not Otherwise Specified (PDD-NOS) describes autism spectrum symptoms which are not clustered to meet the diagnostic requirements of AS or HFA. So although it cannot be said that the person definitely has AS or HFA, he will have a significant number of features which correspond with ASD spectrum. This is another 'not the usual picture' label. It is more often used with children, and is now considered rather dated diagnostic practice, but you may find this label applied to a parent who was diagnosed before 2013.

Classic autism is usually associated with the severe end of the spectrum. Symptoms are noticed early on and are obvious. The triad of impairments is present and may include particularly rigid behaviour, self-harm, social withdrawal, repetitive speech and obsessive behaviour. Although it may occur in individuals with average intelligence, classic autism is usually associated with a learning disability.

What does this mean for the individual?

A diagnosis of ASD of whatever type will have a number of shared difficulties, which will vary in severity, depending on their particular profile. We have said that these are focussed on the triad of impairments and additional sensory sensitivities and needs with respect to routine. In everyday life, a number of likely areas of difficulty can be identified:

Social communication

People with ASD have difficulty understanding social language (even though they may be able to define what words mean). These social language difficulties include:

- interpreting non-verbal communication: gestures, facial expressions or tone of voice
- managing social eye contact: for example, focussing on a person's mouth, avoiding eye contact, making too much eye contact by staring or using unusual glances instead of the usual conversational rhythm of looking and glancing away
- knowing how to manage conversations with others: starts and ends, turn taking and choosing appropriate subjects (sometimes they turn conversations into a monologue)
- making small talk and social chit-chat
- picking up social hints and cues
- using complex words and phrases which are almost, but not quite, on subject
- emotional expression, with what is said not matching what is felt
- literal understanding with varied understanding of jokes, metaphor and sarcasm

- being undiplomatic and, as a result, being regarded as tactless or unnecessarily blunt.

Social relationships

Problems with understanding how relationships are formed and maintained means that people with ASD may be affected in the following ways:

- They may struggle to make and maintain friendships, risking loneliness and depression.

- They may not understand the unwritten 'social rules' that most of us learn throughout childhood and well into adulthood. Rules such as not making personal comments, the difference between work behaviour and social behaviour, and what to do on a date are likely to be misunderstood or only partly observed.

- Because of this lack of understanding, they may behave in an eccentric or seemingly inappropriate manner.

- They may desire close relationships, but not be able to establish and maintain these.

- They may find other people's behaviour and responses changeable, random and ultimately confusing.

- They may seem socially withdrawn, aloof or bored.

- They can appear to have no interest in other people and their concerns.

- They can be vulnerable to exploitation.

Social imagination

Saying that people with ASD have social imagination difficulties does not mean that they completely lack imagination; many are very artistic, musical or literate. However, people with ASD can have difficulty with situations which require socially based imagination. This includes:

- predicting what is likely to happen in a social situation – thinking 'If I do this, then x is likely to happen'

- imagining alternative outcomes to social situations – thinking 'If I do this then x, y, or z might happen'

- being able to generate an understanding of the thoughts or feelings of others from their behaviour, and then being able to predict what they might do

- having a limited understanding that other people do not have access to the same information as you – for example, talking to someone assuming that they have the same knowledge about a topic as you

- having a limited understanding that others have a different perspective on life from your own

- difficulty resolving conflict

- difficulty understanding why they should conform

- a tendency to be rigid and lack flexibility, preferring routine activities or those rooted in logic and systems

- having narrow interests and limited tolerance for unrelated matters

- a need for routines as routines, rules and rituals help to make the world a more predictable place for the person with ASD; changing these routines may lead to anything from mild anxiety to a full 'meltdown', such as going on holiday, coming home to find the furniture moved round or a bus being late

- repetitive and routine behaviours, such as walking in a specific pattern or insisting on eating the same meal every day to reduce anxiety and the risk of the unknown.

Special interests

These interests can be intense and even become obsessive and all-encompassing. Interests may be lifelong or change from time to time, with people amassing a high level of knowledge about a particular subject. Sometimes interests can be incorporated into a lifestyle (e.g. identification of birds into a birdwatching hobby or an interest in languages into work as a translator); sometimes they can interfere with life (e.g. playing a computer game long into the night).

Sensory difficulties

Both oversensitivity and undersensitivity can occur in any one of the senses (touch, taste, sight, sound or smell). For people who are oversensitive, specific stimuli may be perceived as heightened, disturbing, unpleasant or painful. As the perception of sensory stimuli is extreme, people with oversensitivity can become overloaded with information and have difficulty coping with the feelings generated. People who are undersensitive are receiving too little information, which may lead to increased risk in everyday life. For example, they may not feel pain in the same way as others, leading to an increased risk of injury; they may not hear certain noises well – in the case of traffic this could be hazardous; if they have limited body awareness, they may bump into things, have a poor sense of personal space and have difficulty with fine motor tasks.

Some people use the term *sensory processing disorder* (SPD) to describe this misinterpretation of sensory information.

Additional problems

Approximately 70% of people with ASD also have additional physical or mental health problems, but these are often unrecognized and undiagnosed – as a consequence they go untreated. Problems that may co-occur with ASD include epilepsy, anxiety, depression, problems with attention, dyspraxia, motor coordination problems, gastro-intestinal problems, sleep difficulties, eating disorders, self-injury and anger-based behaviour. These will have an additional impact on an individual's ability to cope with his life and add to the complexity of individual needs.

Heritability and prevalence

The exact mechanism for inheritance of ASD is not well understood. Recent studies have identified two types of families who have members with ASD. One type of family (simplex) has only one family member with ASD and no other diagnoses. This may be due to 'one-off' changes in the DNA sequence and accounts for 19% of diagnoses. The other type of family (multiplex) have one or more family members with a diagnosis and several family members with clear ASD traits. This is more likely to be associated with specific gene traits passed down through generations. We do know that ASD is more likely to be diagnosed in males than females, with a ratio of 4:1 males:females. However, it has recently been recognized that there is some under-diagnosis in the female population as the social difficulties may be masked by female aptitude for social behaviour.

Prevalence studies generally suggest an occurrence rate of 1% of the population in childhood and 1.1% in adults (Brugha *et al.*, 2012). A recent study looking at worldwide occurrence of ASD (Baxter *et al.*, 2015) concluded that prevalence had remained constant worldwide, with little regional variation between 1990 and 2010. They gave a higher prevalence rate of 1 in 132 persons.

Studies also suggest that a significant proportion of people remain undiagnosed, perhaps because up to 80% of adults who are seeking a diagnosis find this process difficult or impossible (Taylor and Marrable, 2011).

Development

Often ASD symptoms can be identified early on, by parents, community health workers or nursery staff. Even if a diagnosis in childhood is not considered, a later review of the person's developmental history is likely to reveal early social difficulties. The average age of diagnosis of ASD is around six years of age; AS tends to be diagnosed much later, at 14 years of age when the increased social demands of secondary school place greater demand on the individual to conform and cope socially. At this stage in life, some young people are beginning to cope with a sense of difference, isolation and social anxiety, and are experiencing bullying. This can lead to low mood, depression and suicidal thinking (Tantam, 2000).

Some people are not diagnosed in their early to mid teens, probably because they have been in an environment (school and family) which has tolerated and adapted to unusual behaviours. Later trigger points for diagnosis are during late teens and early adulthood, when the transition to adult life and expectations (going to university, starting work) places more pressure on the individual. Later still, difficulties in adult life, such as problems at work, with a partner or with relationships generally, may lead an individual, sometimes prompted by a partner, to seek diagnosis. A confounding issue with late diagnosis, particularly where the ASD presentation is either subtle or particularly complex, is that the ASD diagnosis may have been overlooked and symptoms misdiagnosed as depression, personality disorder, psychosis or schizophrenia.

Parents with ASD

Simply by looking at prevalence figures for ASD, we know that there are many established families where one or both parents have ASD traits, if not a full diagnosis. So, having a diagnosis of ASD does not prevent successful parenting, but it may introduce some potential difficulties, particularly if the parent has a complex profile of additional problems. Difficulties identified in adults with ASD may be intensified by the parenting role, with vulnerability to:

- increased psychological distress, with secondary mood disorders such as anxiety or depression (Cederlund, Hagberg and Gillberg, 2010) and in some cases self-harm and suicidal ideation (Punshon, Skirrow and Murphy, 2009)

- victimization by peers (Punshon *et al.*, 2009) and feeling stigmatized (Clarke and van Amerom, 2008)

- worries about what others might think of them (Hurlbutt and Chalmers, 2002).

In addition, parents with ASD may:

- find the intensity of a formal assessment hard to understand and deal with

- lack highly specific skills which you may have assumed they will have

- have difficulty managing their emotions

- have dominant special interests

- find the overall planning and organization required overwhelming

- get stuck on one set of problems and then ruminate about them without finding a solution

- have difficulty understanding what is relevant and what is redundant in terms of detail or knowledge

- have dominant sensory sensitivities

- find dealing with the unexpected alarming

- struggle to understand that their child's thoughts, feelings and needs are different from their own.

They will need to work with professionals who are ASD-aware.

ASD and learning disability

ASD is often seen in people with a learning disability. Asperger syndrome is sometimes diagnosed in people with mild learning disability. The triad of impairments will still apply, but will be intensified by the individual's learning disability. As with people with no learning disability, a clear diagnosis and description of the person's particular symptoms and requirements is important. A speech and language therapy report, which will give details of communication strengths and weaknesses, will also be helpful. The person's profile of need and support requirements prior to becoming a parent, with particular reference to the key traits, will be important determinants of the direction of assessment and assistance.

Diagnosis and treatment

The Autism Act (2009) required local authorities to develop a health and social care strategy for the provision of services to people with ASD. Despite this, service provision remains highly variable; such specialist services that are available are vulnerable to falling victim to local cost savings.

Formal diagnosis can be difficult to source, particularly in adulthood. A few areas have a dedicated service for ASD, which has a diagnostic pathway. In other areas, it is a question of finding a psychiatrist or clinical psychologist with a particular interest in the subject and the additional qualifications for diagnosis.

Recognition for a diagnostic and treatment pathway for children is perhaps more ingrained in service provision. A large percentage of children are diagnosed early on in their lives, but those with less obvious symptoms can remain undiagnosed into adulthood. For children, a specialist integrated autism team with specific skills is required by the Autism Act. This usually consists of paediatricians and/or child and adolescent psychiatrists; speech and language therapists; clinical and/or educational psychologists with additional access to paediatric neurologists, occupational therapists and other specialist professionals. For adults, the recommended team includes clinical psychologists; primary care services; nurses; occupational therapists; psychiatrists; social workers; speech and language therapists; additional support staff to support access to housing, employment and other relevant services.

Bob's story

Jen and Bob had been together for 15 years, having five children during that time. Jen had always done most of the child care, even though, latterly, Bob had been at home all day. Bob worked as a cleaner for ten years, but was sacked when a new boss changed the staff shifts and Bob could not keep up with the time schedule.

Bob now spends most of his time in his shed repairing electrical items, with mixed success. Jen doesn't worry about this; in many respects Bob is just like his father. She is, however, worried about Bob's behaviour when they argue – it seems to be getting worse. All their married lives, when they had a row, Bob would quickly become inarticulate and frustrated. Recently, he had been lashing out at Jen too. Now the kids were older, he was showing signs of doing the same with the teenagers.

One evening, Jen and Bob saw a programme about Asperger syndrome on the TV. Jen realized the people on the programme were just like Bob. Jen talked to a friend at the community centre about this; they helped Jen use the computer to get in touch with a local branch of the National Autistic Society (NAS). They talked to Jen and explained how their support services worked and sent her some leaflets to read. They also advised Jen and Bob how to arrange an assessment. Bob wasn't sure he wanted to do this, but Jen persuaded him.

Bob was diagnosed with AS. He and Jen went to an NAS group session which helped them understand the diagnosis. Bob and Jen talked together about Bob's anger. Jen realized just how important Bob's routines were and that, when angry, he would easily feel overloaded and unable to manage his emotions. She understood that Bob wasn't just being aggressive; he really couldn't cope. They agreed that Bob would go out to his shed to cool off when he was angry. Things have improved since then and Bob feels he is beginning to handle his anger. Jen feels she has a better understanding of why Bob does the things he does.

Diagnosis

NICE (2012) describes best practice in the assessment and diagnosis of ASD as being comprehensive, team-based and carried out by professionals with specific skills in this area. A consideration of early development should form part of the assessment, using an informant (parent, family member or partner) or documentation (e.g. school reports, medical records) where an informant is unavailable.

The use of formal assessment tools is also recommended; these usually require specific training and their use is restricted to a few professional groups (psychiatrists, clinical psychologists and others) and are:

- the Adult Asperger Assessment (AAA) (Baron-Cohen *et al.*, 2005)

- the Asperger Syndrome (and high-functioning autism) Diagnostic Interview (ASDI) (Gillberg, Rastam and Wentz *et al.*, 2001)

- the Ritvo Autism Asperger Diagnostic Scale – Revised (RAADS-R) (Ritvo *et al.*, 2011)

- the Diagnostic Interview for Social and Communication Disorders (DISCO) (Wing, 2003)

- the Autism Diagnostic Interview – Revised (ADI-R) (Lord *et al.*, 1997)

- the Autism Diagnostic Observation Schedule – Generic (ADOS-G) (Lord, 2000).

The last three instruments are suitable for use with people with a learning disability.

In the event of any disagreement about the diagnosis, whether this is disagreement with the individual concerned, his family or involved professionals, a second opinion should be sought. Although research evidence does not support the routine use of biological tests, genetic tests or neuroimaging, they could be included in the case of unresolved disagreement about a diagnosis, or highly complex cases.

During a thorough assessment, the following should be investigated:

- Early development and history, although, depending on the circumstances of each person, an informant who is able to give a perspective on him as he grew up may not be available. Parents are obvious informants, although siblings, friends and other relatives may be used. Medical notes and school reports can be of some help when no other sources are available.

- Physical and mental health history.

- Core signs and symptoms corresponding to the triad of impairments, looking at the development from childhood into adulthood.

- Everyday functioning, strengths and difficulties.

- Sensory sensitivities.

- Behavioural history, current and past difficulties.

- A consideration of risk and any safeguarding issues.

Following diagnosis, a feedback meeting should be held, with attention paid to support needs and additional concerns. Sometimes having a diagnosis and being able to access literature/websites is sufficient help. Other people with ASD will have a range of requirements from social support (e.g. with housing problems) to treatment of co-existing mental health problems (accessed from mainstream mental health services). GPs will be able to offer pharmacological treatment of low mood and anxiety or refer on to appropriate specialists.

Working with parents who have ASD

Research into the best ways of working with people who are on the autism spectrum concludes that interventions with a clear structure are most likely to be effective. Within this structure there are two key principles on which work should be planned:

1. an understanding of the usual patterns of thinking in ASD

2. recognition of the individual's skills, areas of special interest and personal vulnerabilities.

Susan's story

People working with Susan were concerned about the state of her flat. It was so cluttered that it was difficult to clean, with dangerously toppling piles of boxes, books and bags of clothes. If asked, Susan said she was in the process of sorting through everything, but never managed to get rid of anything at all. Instead, she added more.

Susan became pregnant and was allocated a social worker. The social worker looked at Susan's records. Susan was obviously clever; she knew lots of facts about the world and was brilliant at quizzes, but had never done well at school. She had even attended a special school for a short while. The social worker asked Susan if she could meet Susan's mum to gather some background information. Susan's mum chatted about Susan's early life, explaining that Susan had been very close to her younger sister. This sister had always taken the role of 'looking after' Susan, and when her sister had moved to Australia four years ago, Susan had been very withdrawn for some time. Susan's mother remembered that the school had mentioned something about ASD, but nothing had ever come of it. The social worker asked why this had been suggested; Susan's mother talked about Susan's interest in nature, which became almost an obsession at one point, but had been diverted into the study of biology at school.

The social worker helped Susan arrange for an ASD diagnostic assessment through her GP. It took a long time for an appointment, but Susan was finally given a positive diagnosis of AS. Everyone, including Susan, felt they could understand her behaviour much better. Using Susan's interest in biology, the social worker talked to her about child development and safety, and how children need a safe space to play and learn. Susan's mum asked her sister to Skype from Australia to help persuade Susan to use her garage for storage. Gradually, the piles have begun to diminish, but it is a work in progress, needing continued input from all concerned.

Patterns of thinking in ASD

The patterns of thinking we are considering here are neurologically based problems, usually problems with processing information which will have an effect on everyday behaviour. Even if the person you are working with has a sophisticated vocabulary and speaks fluently and well, subtle communication processing difficulties may lead to difficulties such as understanding a long-winded explanation or a discussion from a case conference.

Concrete understanding of language is another area of conversational complexity. People with ASD tend to understand words as having one meaning only and do not 'get' differences in emphasis. This means that colloquial speech and variations in meaning can add to misunderstanding. The simplest way of getting over these communication confusions is to make greater use of visual information, either at the same time as verbal information is given or instead of verbal information.

Using visual information

Visual information can take a number of forms. The most straightforward is written information, particularly useful as parents within this group are likely to have a good range of literacy skills (although make sure you check this first!). You can either provide the information yourself or, if it is practicable, encourage the parent to write (on paper or electronically) his own notes, lists, schedules or directions. Information can be downloaded from the internet, but do make sure you check it first to make sure that the level of language is appropriate for your parent and that the message given is consistent. Other kinds of visual information are photos, pictures, drawings or symbols.

You will find visual information particularly useful when the person is overwhelmed or upset. At these times it is best to minimize verbal content and emphasize the visual aspect.

Social Stories™

Social Stories™ were developed by Carol Gray in 1991 to help with social understanding. They are short and simple guides which provide consistent information on a single topic, designed to prepare the individual for a particular situation, prompt socially appropriate behaviour and give a perspective on the thoughts or emotions of others. Social Stories™ usually *label* what is happening, *explain* why they happen and *clarify* what the expected reaction or behaviour should be. They are usually written around individual needs and could contain words only, pictures only or a mix of both (Gray, 2015). Parent and professionals can read the stories together as many times as needed, discuss the situation and the story remains as a consistent prompt. Social Stories™ can be used in a variety of situations – for example:

- to explain why making sure your child eats vegetables is important

- to prepare for a visit to the hospital to see a paediatrician

- to list things to do when attending a mother and toddler group

- to explain what is likely to happen at court during care proceedings.

Comic Strip Conversations™

Carol Gray then went on to develop the idea of Comic Strip Conversations™, again designed to support social understanding. Comic Strip Conversations™ are simple visual representations of conversations, usually using simple stick figures. They use colour to illustrate different feelings such as red for angry, blue for sad. Comic Strip Conversations™ show what is said in the conversation or interaction, how the different people might be feeling and what they are thinking or intending. They help to set interactions in an overall social context and slow down what has happened, which allows time for verbal processing. They can be used to explain:

- specific social skills – for example, the volume used to speak in different places/environments

- important information, such as what will happen at a meeting

- people's perspectives, feelings and ideas

- misunderstandings that have arisen as part of an interaction.

Circle of friends

The term *circle of friends* in this context is different from the circle of support idea often seen when planning community-based support networks for people with a learning disability. It is used here to explain differences in relationships and the behavioural codes that relate to these differences. To use this technique (Attwood, 1999), concentric circles are drawn with the person in the centre. As the circles move outwards and away from the person, so relationships become more distant, and different kinds of behaviour and behavioural expectations apply.

Non-verbal communication

People with ASD usually have some degree of difficulty in interpreting non-verbal communication as in body language, tone of voice, facial expression, gestures, posture, personal space, eye gaze and general appearance (Wood, 2010). We use non-verbal language in a number of ways: to express emotions, interpersonal attitudes and personality, and to accompany speech – it helps us manage conversation and to mark rituals such as greeting and parting. In addition, subtle relationships such as power and influence are also expressed non-verbally. Experts typically say that between 80 and 90% of our communication is non-verbal; so, if this area is something of a mystery to a parent, our verbal communication must be particularly clear and thorough, and non-verbal elements controlled. Explanations and instructions must be explicit, not implied. You must not try to interpret the feelings, mood or attitude of a parent with ASD based on his body language.

Behaviour

Behaviourally based difficulties, such as breaking agreements, having a 'meltdown' or general non-compliance are more likely to be linked with ASD-specific problems than a wish to be oppositional. For example, if you do not understand a person's sensory sensitivity to noise and meet in a busy café, that meeting will be unsatisfactory. The message here is that circumstances and environments should be adapted as far as possible to meet the parents' needs, rather than confronting mild obsessions, phobias and habits 'head on'.

Ben's story

An assessment interview with Ben, a parent with ASD, was set up in a room at a children's centre. Ben was familiar with the centre, but this room contained an examination couch; this suggested medical interventions to Ben and made him very frightened so that he could hardly speak. Ben appeared to be uncooperative and almost aggressive. Luckily, part of the way through the interview, Ben felt confident enough to explain his worries, and the room was changed with the result that Ben was able to be himself and demonstrate his skills as a parent much better.

Problem solving

Working out what to do in a social situation is likely to challenge people with ASD. If the situation is unstructured and has no clear rules, it is very difficult to understand what the response should be. In this situation, extra explicit information is needed in order to explain the 'unwritten rules'. For example, knowing how to deal with a parents' evening at school can be confusing for anyone. The parent with ASD who has difficulty understanding the social and situational cues (staff sitting at desks with a spare chair, seeing other parents queueing), and does not know how to ask for help, may well simply turn around and walk out, unable to cope with the anxiety. He then risks being considered by teaching staff as a parent who is not interested in his child's progress. Prior preparation, perhaps with the use of a social story, would help to manage this kind of situation.

Sensory sensitivities

Many (but not all) people with ASD have a highly individual response to sensory stimulation. Sometimes it can be quite disabling, in a way that you might not expect or predict, as ordinary experiences are perceived as highly (even unbearably) intense. Common sensitivities are to sound and touch, but taste, light, intensity, colours and smell can also be involved. Reverse reactions to pain and temperature are also seen, where the person appears to have a high threshold to pain or heat (Attwood, 1999). Some people learn to cope with their sensitivities by blocking the source of the problem – for example, humming in response to a particular noise. As suggested, the environment can be adapted – for example, by a partner being responsible for vacuuming when the partner with ASD who cannot stand the noise of the vacuum cleaner is out. Social Stories™ can be used to explain the source and likely duration of a stimulation (the fan in a room comes on when you go in but will switch itself off after two minutes). In general, you need to identify sensitivities and incorporate these as a need in any work undertaken. Regard them as part of the person and respect that person's individuality.

Rachel's story

Rachel had a diagnosis of ASD and learning difficulties. She was managing her life well following the birth of her baby with her partner, Steven. Recently, Steven had reported a concern to the social worker. Rachel had been walking out of the house whenever the baby was distressed, leaving Steven to cope alone, often not returning for some time.

The social worker talked to Rachel and Steven about this. Rachel said that she couldn't stand the noise of the baby crying – it felt like a sharp pain in her head. Steven said that he knew Rachel had always been sensitive to noises like the vacuum cleaner and planes flying overhead.

Rachel remembered using a graduated approach to help her cope with the noise of the vacuum cleaner, starting with it a long way away from her and slowly moving closer. Together they worked out how this could be used with the baby; the social worker suggested having ear plugs as a back-up. They worked systematically through an agreed plan. Now Rachel is much better and able to cope with all but the worst crying.

Organization

Problems with the management and organization of tasks are often associated with ASD. This will affect parents as they are responsible for organizing not only themselves but their children too, as well as the additional demands that go along with having contact with a number of professionals. Problems may be seen at each stage of a task – that is, with initiation (or starting off), carrying out the task and generalizing what has been learned to other similar situations. The most effective way of working with people who have ASD is first to aim to increase the clarity of the task, making sure that what is expected is precisely understood, and, second, to increase the consistency or predictability of a task using written calendars, lists or schedules. The ideas on helping parents with borderline learning disabilities explained in Chapter 3 can be applied; you will just have to check that they are meaningful for the individual and that they are presented in an acceptable visual format. Different kinds of organizational aids are:

- *A time-based schedule*: it covers a period of time, such as a half-day, day or week, and lists activities in time order. The amount of detail will vary with the parent's needs; reminders can be added, such as 'bring developmental record' for an appointment with the health visitor.

- *Lists and schedules relating to one activity*: this is designed to help with sequential organization, covering the 'what, where, when and how much' of a particular task. So the task is described, including how you know when you are finished and how to monitor progress. It can be detailed or a brief list to act as a reminder or record.

- *Good visual support*: the need to accompany verbal information with visual information has been emphasized in the early part of this chapter. For parents with organizational difficulties, attention must be paid to the clarity of written information, with words well spaced in large print and important points highlighted.

- *Environmental organization*: if a home is chaotic, untidy, unclean or full of hoarded belongings, then family life will be compromised. Parents with ASD may need support with cleaning routines, regular sorting of clutter, developing systems for managing information about the children or the children's school equipment. The kind of help needed will vary tremendously; for example, some parents may be very conscious of cleanliness and germs, but have difficulty finding their child's reading book in the morning.

Individual factors

Within the group of people considered to be on the spectrum, there is enormous variability in cognitive abilities, social understanding, personality and behavioural traits. Amongst parents with ASD, there will be similar variation in the support that may be required, from the person who needs regular support in maintaining his level of functioning, to the adult who manages life reasonably well, merely being considered a little eccentric by friends and neighbours.

Parents should be encouraged to specify their own support needs, being able to describe:

- what is the most helpful form of communication

- where and how they learn best

- sensitive topics

- potential sensory difficulties.

Marital and partner relationships

Partners of people with ASD who are not on the spectrum often find the behaviour, interests and lack of flexibility of their partner difficult to understand. Good explanatory information can be invaluable; the NAS and other local organizations have a number of explanatory leaflets and websites; specialist services may offer 'partner workshops' or a support service; or, if diagnosis is recent, the diagnosing clinician may be prepared to meet with the partner too.

Coordination

Recent efforts have been made to raise awareness of ASD, but not all professionals working with parents will have a working knowledge of what it is likely to mean for families when one (or perhaps both) parents have a diagnosis of ASD. Although support networks should always coordinate information carefully in order to ensure that parents are not confused by differing messages, instructions or advice, this is critical when working with parents with ASD. People with ASD need their lives to be both understandable and predictable. Confusing information will cause additional stress as the parent struggles to reconcile different sources; it may overload individuals and lead to a 'meltdown'. It can be helpful to pre-plan communication systems (e.g. regular email updates between those concerned) and what to do in the event of apparently conflicting advice (e.g. nominating one person as the 'lead' who will act as arbitrator and resolve apparent difficulties).

Summary

The main points of this chapter can be summarized as follows:

- Although there is tremendous variation between people who have a diagnosis of ASD, each person on the spectrum shares common problems with social behaviour, empathy, flexibility and communication, known as the triad of impairments.

- These are likely to be accompanied by repetitive behaviour and sensory sensitivities.

- Historically, a number of sub-diagnoses have been used to describe different 'types' of autism, although the current trend is moving towards an overarching diagnosis of ASD.

- Problems with social communication, social relationships and social imagination are likely to be accompanied by additional mental and physical health problems, which often remain undiagnosed and untreated.

- Difficulties identified in adults with ASD may be intensified by the parenting role, with a number of issues needing to be considered.

- Advice on best practice in the assessment and diagnosis of ASD is set out in the National Institute for Health and Clinical Excellence guidelines (NICE, 2013).

- Research into the best ways of working with people who are on the autism spectrum concludes that interventions with a clear structure are most likely to be effective.

- Work undertaken with parents should also be based on an understanding of the patterns of thinking in ASD and recognition of the individual's skills, areas of special interest and personal vulnerabilities.

- Coordination and communication between professionals themselves as well as with parents should be planned and systematic in order to ensure that messages have a consistent meaning and do not confuse the parent with ASD.

Chapter 6

Parenting, Emotions and Attachment

Rather than the adult–child interaction, this chapter explores the fairly new field of adult attachment in learning disabilities. We focus on:

- early vulnerability

- the context of attachment in learning disability

- the practicalities of working with parents who have a learning disability and attachment issues.

Vulnerability

Many factors that have a negative impact on parenting capacity in the general population will also be relevant where parents have a mild or borderline learning disability. Parental vulnerability associated with a history of early abuse or neglect, a history of institutionalization, mental health or emotional disorders, substance abuse, relationship violence, criminality and negative attitudes towards parenting has been well established (Cleaver, Unell and Aldgate, 1999). These factors continue to apply where a parent has a learning disability, with the addition of being educated within the special education sector, but levels of vulnerability are greater. We have seen that people with a learning disability have to contend not only with limitations linked with their cognitive profile but also social problems such as bullying, harassment, social exclusion and reduced opportunities to participate in a full range of life experiences (see Chapter 2). It is also recognized that people with a learning disability have increased emotional vulnerability through raised risk of disrupted attachment relationships and low self-esteem, with resulting poor mental health. The likely development, diagnosis and presentation of mental health disorders is described in Chapter 4, but more generalized emotional difficulties which cannot be given a specific mental health diagnosis need further consideration. These generalized emotional difficulties have a significant impact on parental capacity in terms of the parents' ability to use existing skills abilities and knowledge, to be available to learn new skills and to be able to manage their behaviour as a parent over the longer term. In order to gauge the influence of an individual's emotional development on her current behaviour and capacity, it is helpful to use an attachment perspective.

Attachment

Attachment is the enduring emotional bond that arises early in life between children and their main caregivers. These early experiences have a profound influence, affecting relationship style and psychological adjustment throughout our lives.

Forming secure attachments is important for the development of positive self-esteem and personal autonomy. Experiencing a secure attachment allows the individual to develop an understanding of relationships and how they are made, maintained and regulated, and helps to maintain emotional well-being (Carr, 2003). It also allows the individual to begin to develop personal understanding of emotional behaviour, reactions and regulation. However, the development of emotional regulation skills is dependent on the infant having had experience of a regulating relationship with an adult (Golding, 2008).

Secure attachment results when caregivers respond to their child, interpreting her expressed or implicit cues and acting in a positive and protective manner. The child in turn develops an expectation that others will be there for her on a consistent and predictable basis, and that she is loved. If the attachment figure remains unresponsive, secure attachments (and their associated expectations) will not be made or maintained. The child begins to develop emotionally protective strategies which affect the way she deals with relationships; Champion (2010) suggests that patterns of attachment first become evident between nine and 12 months of age.

In these insecure attachment strategies, preoccupation with the relationship, or conversely withdrawal from the relationship, may be seen, and in some cases of severe abuse or neglect contact with the significant other is sought but then rejected when experienced. These strategies may offer the child some emotional protection whilst growing up in a difficult emotional environment. However, if they remain unchanged and continue into adulthood, later adult relationships and subsequent caregiving may be defined in the same way and will not necessarily be either helpful or protective. Insecurity and distress in adult relationships will result in troubled intimate interactions, which in turn reinforce the existing behaviours, thoughts and feelings relating to relationships.

However, attachment styles are not necessarily fixed, and as we develop into adulthood and are exposed to a range of experiences and reflections, these strategies can be modified in the direction of greater security. For example, experiencing a partner relationship which is supportive and mutually responsive can help to change internal models from believing yourself to be unlovable and predicting that your emotional needs will not be met to believing that you are worth loving and that your emotional needs will be met.

Background

Attachment theory was first proposed by John Bowlby in the 1950s, arising from his observations as a child psychiatrist of emotionally disturbed behaviour in young children. He theorized that early experiences in childhood have an important influence on development and behaviour later in life, viewing attachment in an evolutionary context, as a source of safety and security for the young (Bowlby, 1969).

Ainsworth developed these ideas further, proposing three attachment classifications: secure, insecure avoidant and insecure ambivalent. A later category of disorganized or disoriented attachment was added by Main and Solomon (1986).

As researchers began to identify that relationships between the child and caregiver had a longer-term influence on relationships during adulthood, attachment theory began to be applied to adult behaviour and relationships. During the 1980s, Hazan and Shaver (1994) considered romantic relationships, exploring the nature of couple relationships within an attachment framework. They concluded that although adult attachment styles were not identical to adult partnership styles, very similar principles seemed to be operating. Similarly, Collins and Read (1990) found that positive early attachments related to feelings of security in adulthood, whereas avoidant and anxious early relationships tended to result in adults who were more mistrustful of others. A two-dimensional model of romantic attachment based on anxiety and avoidance was offered by Bartholemew and Horowitz (1991):

- *Low anxiety + low avoidance = secure attachment style*. Once an individual has developed the capacity for secure attachments, she will be likely to continue this pattern into adulthood. In this style, partners have positive views of themselves and of each other. They are able to achieve a balance between closeness and independence, which strengthens rather than undermines the relationship.

- *Low anxiety + high avoidance = dismissing avoidant*. Adults in these relationships appear to have little need for closeness, being emotionally self-sufficient and seeming to avoid intimacy. They are likely to have an internal model with a high regard for the self and low regard of others, including their partners. They deal with rejection by using distancing strategies, minimizing emotional response.

- *High anxiety + low avoidance = anxious preoccupied* (equivalent to Hazan and Shaver's anxious/ambivalent description). Adults with relationships in this category have an internal model with a negative view of the self and a positive view of others. As a consequence, they are likely to be highly anxious and heavily reliant on approval from partners. They actively seek high levels of closeness and may invest time and worry trying to maintain relationships which are not worthwhile or of benefit to themselves.

- *High avoidance + high anxiety = fearful avoidant attachment style.* This style is characterized by adults with internal models featuring negative views of the self and others. They may select partners who are ambivalent about intimacy. Although people in this category desire closeness, once achieved it is difficult to tolerate as they feel vulnerable within intimate relationships. They are likely to be less trusting of partners, at the same time feeling that they do not deserve good treatment themselves.

More recently, Patricia Crittenden, building on the work of Bowlby and Ainsworth, proposed the Dynamic Maturational Model of Attachment and Adaptation (DMM) (Crittenden and Landini, 2011). This model describes attachment strategies that are adaptive as they mature and develop over time. The function of these strategies is protection of the self, with an additional function of protection of future children, thus influencing parenting style. Crittenden proposed three key strategies: avoidant (A), secure (B) and ambivalent/resistant (C). Although the A and C strategies are insecure, they are not necessarily problematic; they only become so if they become overgeneralized over time as they will then be used in inappropriate situations. The model becomes more complex, with a number of sub-types defined. These progress from eight A categories through three B categories and a further eight C categories, with the higher numbers showing deepening of the strategy.

The A strategy reflects care that is predictable but not attuned. The predictability allows the child to develop cause-and-effect thinking, and thoughts (which protect) are prioritized over feelings (which are risky). Although feelings are suppressed and mistrusted, they may sometimes be uncontainable and find expression as sudden outbursts. As the child develops, she becomes more used to separating thoughts and emotions, and more skilled at keeping emotions at a distance. Caretaking, compliance or isolation may be developed as responsive strategies and continue into adult life.

The B strategy is the 'balanced', secure strategy allowing for optimal functioning as a child and adult. The individual is able to act in an adaptive and flexible manner, choosing effective ways of managing emotional threat and reflecting and learning from challenging situations.

The C strategy reflects care that is unpredictable and not reliably attuned. This unpredictability means that the care figure is sometimes there and sometimes not, with no regularity. It leads the child to exaggerate negative emotion in order to make sure her needs are met, with tantrums, weeping and high levels of expression. In order to maintain the carer's attention, emotional patterns are varied, often with charming and disarming behaviour to limit the carer's reaction. Later on, these strategies can include angry, aggressive and punishing behaviours in the adult presentation.

This model also emphasizes the role of life experience, maturation and reflection as well as new relationships. These may all trigger changes (reorganization) in the attachment strategies used by an individual.

Attachment in learning disabilities

Studies on quality of attachment in children with a learning disability (where parents do not have a learning disability) have concluded that parents are less likely to be able to build a secure attachment with their child. Some researchers talk about the 'crisis of diagnosis', where parents' natural reaction of shock can be complicated by the manner in which the news is broken and followed up. Most parents assume that their children will be healthy and develop normally, so being told a child has a learning disability often triggers a process of grief, anger and guilt. It takes time to accept the diagnosis and to mourn the loss of the desired child, which may interfere with early bonding and later attachment formation.

Following the period of diagnosis, with most learning disabilities being identified by the age of five, the characteristics of the child play a role in the attachment cycle. The child with a learning disability is more likely to give unclear signals about her needs, which places additional demands on the parent to be able to interpret and cope with their child's communications. When parents fail to respond appropriately in identifying and meeting their children's needs, Fahlberg (1991) contends that the arousal–relaxation cycle is disrupted. This then disrupts the attachment process, making difficulties in the relationship more likely to occur.

Relationships between the parent and learning-disabled child which are not secure are more often disorganized or atypical, with these relationship types occurring at a similar rate to children who have been brought up in institutions or exposed to trauma. Significant links between carer responsiveness and secure attachment support the application of recognized models of attachment to relationships with children with a learning disability (Feninger-Schaal, 2010). Explanations for the lower rates of secure attachments in children with a learning disability are not conclusive; however, disruption of the parental caregiving system, or the particular combination of cognitive deficits and communication problems have been suggested as potential mechanisms (Bernier and Meins,

2008). Baker *et al.* (2007) point out that, in order to foster positive emotional development in children with a learning disability, it seems that it is possibly more important to establish a secure attachment relationship with carers. Paradoxically, the likelihood of establishing such a relationship is lower than in the non-learning-disabled population of children.

Research on adult attachment in learning disability is limited by the requirement for relatively good communication and verbal understanding skills plus the ability to recall and reflect on a number of experiences and relationships for accurate assessment. However, progress has been made in the development of specialized assessments which can be used to assess attachment and relationship quality in parents with a learning disability. Studies have identified the same range of adult attachment styles in people with mild and moderate learning disabilities as in the general population. In addition, Larson, Alim and Tsakanikos (2011) identified a link between depression and insecure avoidant attachment. Penketh *et al.* (2014) noted that individuals with a learning disability and observed secure attachment styles tended to show lower levels of social avoidance and were less reliant on the approval of others, with the implication that they would be better equipped to develop personal emotional support networks.

Some studies have examined attachment styles amongst people with learning disabilities in more detail. Schuengel *et al.* (2013) were able to apply attachment behaviours, relationships, styles and disorders to a group of people (adults) with learning disabilities. The authors suggested that interventions shown to be effective for children and adults without learning disabilities could be modified and applied to the learning-disabled population as well. The problem here was more likely to be professionals recognizing the need for treatment and the availability of specialist treatment itself inhibiting the development of appropriate methods.

Few studies have explored the attachments made between parents with learning disabilities and their children. Booth and Booth (1998) interviewed 30 adults who had grown up with parents who had a learning disability. They found that the factors which promoted resilience included individual personality characteristics, family dynamics and external supports. Personality-based resilience factors were those associated with secure attachments: sociability, responsiveness, flexibility and a readiness to take on responsibility. Similarly, family dynamics were those which would be expected to foster secure attachments: expressed warmth, stability and security. Support from the wider social network was more likely to be achieved by people with reciprocal social relationships, confidence and self-esteem, again reflecting secure attachment.

Perkins *et al.* (2002) considered the interaction between the child's perception of stigma and attachment. Thirty-six children and adolescents of mothers with a learning disability participated in the study. Whilst the authors recognized that the mother's behaviour was important, they emphasized that the child's perception of the parent was also a critical factor in the formation and maintenance of attachment relationships. Perception of the mother as a cold or ambivalent caregiver correlated with a high perception of stigma and less secure attachment. Children with an avoidant attachment style in particular tended to have low self-esteem. The study concluded that assisting the mother to provide warm and attuned caregiving was a valuable use of resources, as was helping the older child develop a rounded view of him/herself as a person with a number of skills and abilities.

Granqvist *et al.* (2014) commented that attachments between parents with a learning disability and their children is a particularly important subject area for research as a child's attachment is often referred to in evaluations of parental competence. Secure attachment is viewed as positive and protective, and insecure or disorganized attachment as indicative of vulnerabilities and difficulties for both parent and child. The quality of attachment between parent and child directly reflects quality of care, with secure attachment associated with attuned and skilled care, and insecure attachment associated with care at least lacking attunement or even directly harmful.

Grandqvist and colleagues explored attachment in a group of mothers with learning disabilities. The importance of context was emphasized in this study, as it was evident that the group of mothers had histories showing very high rates of abuse, trauma and maltreatment when compared with the matched sample of non-learning-disabled mothers. When variables such as presence or absence of the father and mother's and child's intelligence levels were separated out, this experience of abuse, trauma and maltreatment linked with higher rates of insecure or disorganized attachment with the child. The suggested mechanism was that the mothers with a traumatic history had fewer internal and external resources and supports to help resist or repair the effects of trauma, particularly when the trauma was associated with attachment figures. The emphasis is that it is the trauma rather than the mother's learning disability that increases risk to the child.

The authors also noted the implication that an element of resilience in the children of mothers with a learning disability must be implied by the fact that a substantial proportion of the children demonstrated secure attachments with their mothers.

Laura's story

Laura had an early history of living with a mother who had severe depression and an alcoholic stepfather. Her stepfather would often come home drunk and beat Laura's mother and occasionally Laura and her younger sister too.

Laura attended special school with a boarding facility; following a case conference, it was decided that Laura would become a weekly boarder, going home at weekends. When Laura was 14, she was sexually abused by one of the evening staff. He told Laura not to tell anyone as no one would believe her and she would be put in a 'home' for telling lies. The only way Laura could cope with everything that was happening was to try not to think about it and get through life as best as she could.

Laura left school at 16 and began a relationship with an older man who was a friend of the family. This was a sexual relationship from the start; Laura thought that was what relationships were like, and she quickly found she was pregnant. Laura's 'boyfriend' disappeared and her father told her to leave home. Laura's social worker arranged temporary accommodation for her, then a move to a mother-and-baby unit. At the unit, Laura showed that she had learned to look after herself practically (cooking, cleaning and personal care) whilst boarding. However, it soon became clear that Laura actively sought sexual attention from men as a way of feeling wanted and important. Scratches were noticed on Laura's arms and sometimes, after meals, her room smelt of vomit. Staff were highly concerned about Laura's behaviour. She was referred to the local Learning Disability Team and diagnosed with probable PTSD, moderate depression and a possible eating disorder. Antidepressant medication helped; Laura was offered counselling but refused to engage. She said she 'had stopped thinking about bad things' and did not want it all brought up again. Assessment of Laura continues, but staff are very concerned about her ability to understand about the need to protect herself and her baby, and her ability to manage her emotional state. To introduce the idea of therapy, Laura is having regular 'chats' with a trusted member of staff during which they talk about everyday events combined with a little reflection on the past. This is supervised by a psychologist from the community team; it is hoped that Laura will agree to a more formal therapy arrangement soon, although it is recognized that major change in Laura's behaviour may not happen in time for her to parent her baby safely.

Working with adults with a learning disability and attachment issues

There is no one answer to the question of 'How do I work with a parent who has attachment problems?' as this will vary with each individual's history, experiences, belief system, personality and learning style. If the attachment issues are long-standing, complex and resistant to resolution, then professional support will be the best course of action. However, where a parent appears to have attachment issues which, although apparent, do not dominate her everyday life, interactions that are attachment-sensitive will help to establish and maintain engagement.

A consideration when working with parents who have a learning disability is emotional maturity. In learning disability, emotional development can be significantly slowed, such that the adolescent period extends to at least the mid-20s, and some people will feature emotional immaturity as an enduring part of their profile. Interactions should be consistent with the person's developmental age; be aware that the emotional development of young parents who have a learning disability may not reflect their chronological age, so that interactions and expectations should be paced accordingly.

A parent who has experienced a number of negative life events will often have poor understanding of the concept of family life. Her internal models of how families work are likely to be skewed, resulting in limited understanding of the parenting role, boundary setting and the ability to recognize when help is needed. A parent with a learning disability who has problems in this area will need to have these complex concepts broken down, explained, actions agreed and changes in behaviour supported.

A negative sense of self-worth is often associated with early neglect or emotional abuse. In earlier chapters, we have seen that people with learning disabilities are more vulnerable to these negative experiences and the resulting emotional difficulties. The intrinsic message of these experiences is 'I am not worthwhile/I am bad/something is wrong with me', resulting in a range of behavioural responses from low mood and self-harm to acting out and aggression. Addressing significantly negative beliefs is best tackled through a formal therapeutic relationship. A parent can be supported to begin to build self-belief and self-esteem when this is a part of their presentation which impedes progress rather than a significant therapeutic issue. Some ideas relating to low self-esteem are covered in Chapter 3.

Attachment styles and potential presentations

The parents' attachment style in itself may present a number of challenges to intervention. Sometimes consideration of where the parent is from an attachment perspective may help to focus your choices with respect to working with parents.

Parents with a *dismissing avoidant* attachment style may:

- Show an apparent indifference to new and demanding situations. Deny the need for support and help. Making support a matter of course at first, allowing early success will allow a trusting relationship to be built.

- Need to be autonomous and resent direction. Showing that you wish to work collaboratively and positively will help to avoid activating negative behaviour.

- Underachieve and have a limited use of creativity.

- Work better initially with a task focus where the task acts as an emotional safety net. Have a clear start and end point, an agreement about what is to be done and everything ready before you begin.

Parents in the *fearful avoidant* attachment group may:

- Need to feel safe in order to reduce anxiety. This is important, as anxiety impairs learning, progress and change. You may need to introduce specific anxiety-reducing exercises at the beginning of each session or simply take time to get to know the parent (familiarity reducing anxiety). Find out from the parent what makes her feel safe and introduce these features into your work.

Parents in the *anxious preoccupied* attachment group may:

- Become more controlling as they become more anxious. You will need to address anxiety by introducing specific anxiety-reducing exercises or structuring sessions as initially very 'safe' and predictable, gradually introducing challenge.

- Be unwilling to accept the need to take new ideas on board. Work from a positive stance – together draw up a list of strengths, 'what I can do', and add things to do to make this even better.

- Find admitting to not being able to do something humiliating or worrying. Take the worry away by asking the parent to set her own goals and choose what she wishes to do or discuss. If there are areas that must be tackled, use a stance of revision ('let's just go over this') and joint discussion.

- Need reliable and predictable routines, but build in some allowance for flexibility.

Taking a more general view, the following points are relevant for parents with learning disabilities who have attachment issues:

- They may place a negative interpretation on neutral non-verbal behaviour and verbal communication. You must be explicit and consider whether what you have said is open to misinterpretation. Check back with the parents on their understanding of what you have said.

- From past experience, parents may be more used to negative feedback and attention; they may not be used to responding to praise and approval, and instead look for the negative. Work with these parents to help them accept positives and remember and recall achievements.

- Again, due to past experience, parents may not recognize when they have achieved something, instead focussing on a small 'wrong' detail. After learning to accept praise, helping parents learn to recognize when they have reached a goal or made a positive step, and to praise themselves will help to maintain progress in the long term.

- They may have difficulty with internal emotional regulation and may suddenly respond with a seemingly out-of-the-blue outburst which, in fact, relates to internal thoughts or feelings. Discussion of a parent's internal thoughts can help to establish a clearer understanding between parents and those offering support.

- They may appear easily overwhelmed as their emotional difficulties limit their ability to use coping strategies; sensitivity to the amount of information or discussion a parent is able to manage at one time will help diffuse these feelings

- They may appear controlling, a habit which has developed as a result of experiences with untrustworthy or absent carers. It is particularly important with parents who feel this way that you are able to demonstrate availability and reliability, by keeping appointments as arranged and following through agreed actions.

- They may be anxious and fearful. High levels of anxiety will impair learning, or anxiety may be manifested as apparent opposition ('if I say no to this I won't have to try it'). Calming techniques such as managing the amount of stimulation in the environment (noise, visitors and interruptions), making the pattern of visits predictable and behaving in a calm and containing manner yourself will all help to reduce anxiety levels.

- They may be overly active or talkative as a way of blocking bad thoughts. This is something you could discuss with the parent, but if her emotional state is overwhelming, specialist support is likely to be needed.

- They may appear to be highly dependent on the interest and attention of professionals in order to engage and learn, and lose focus when attention is withdrawn. Many professionals are in their job because they wish to support people and help them progress. But it is important to recognize that dependence on you, whilst it can be flattering, does not aid independence. A parent who has difficulty managing without emotional attention and support must be encouraged to do so by taking very gradual steps towards a specific goal, helping her to recognize small steps as an achievement.

- They are likely to have problems with building security and associated anxiety. This can be addressed with the introduction of elements of structure and routine. You can introduce predictability into your visits so that the parent has an idea of what is likely to happen or be discussed over time. You can also help to introduce structure and routine into her home life by jointly planning routines and activities.

- They may overreact to correction or implied criticism. This is a very sensitive area for the parent with attachment difficulties. Any negatives are likely to be understood by the parent in an exaggerated form and the accompanying sense of shame may also be disproportionately felt. You must use attuned and reflective language which demonstrates an understanding of how the parent feels and the support that you are able to offer.

- They may overreact when things go wrong. You must act as a containing influence, being reassuring and caring, present to support rather than take over.

- They may lack positive models in their life. Make sure you are a positive emotional model, coping with difficulties calmly, acknowledging mistakes and maintaining a positive manner.

Mel's story

Mel had been progressing well at the family centre, attending all her sessions and seeming to enjoy meeting other mums. Suddenly, she stopped going, and no one could understand why. If asked, Mel said, 'I don't need their help'.

The group leader visited Mel to find out more about her lack of attendance. They talked about how Mel had been brought up and about Mel's relationship with her mother. Mel described her as a 'wonderful' mother, who had strict rules which Mel obeyed; otherwise her mother would not speak to her. Mel thought that this had been 'for her own good' and that she had learned to behave well as a result. Mel remembered other people described her as 'very grown up' for her age; 'I learned to take care of myself early on,' Mel said. Although a loner as a child, Mel had made a few friends and, she felt, had a good relationship with her partner. Talking about the group, Mel said that she had got on well with the other mums until at one of the sessions her son fell over and Mel encouraged him to get up and carry on playing. One of the other mums told Mel she should have given him a cuddle. Mel felt criticized, embarrassed and ashamed – her solution to this was to withdraw from the group and 'manage by herself'. The group leader helped Mel to think about why she had reacted in this way. They agreed that maybe Mel had needed more cuddles in her life as she grew up and wanted to give this to her son, but found it hard to show her emotions. They also agreed that the other mum should not have spoken to Mel as she did (it was in the 'group rules' to be positive), but perhaps Mel had overreacted by withdrawing from the group. They agreed that Mel would come back for another session, and that just before the group began, the two mums would meet so that Mel could say what she felt (helped by the group leader). When they met, the other mum apologized, saying she 'hadn't meant anything by it' and that Mel was a 'great mum'. Mel continued to attend the group, getting better at talking about how she felt and giving her son cuddles.

Summary

This chapter can be summarized as follows:

- An attachment perspective is helpful when trying to understand the vulnerabilities associated with having a learning disability.

- In order to foster positive emotional development in children with a learning disability, it seems that the attachment relationship is particularly important but, paradoxically, the likelihood of establishing such a relationship appears to be lower than in the non-learning-disabled population of children.

- Research on adult attachment in learning disabilities is beginning to identify the same range of attachment styles as in the general population, suggesting that assessments and interventions used with the non-learning-disabled population could be adapted for use with people with learning disabilities.

- A recent study of attachment relationships between mothers with a learning disability and their children identified a substantial proportion of relationships within the secure category. The experience of abuse, trauma and maltreatment was very much higher in the group of mothers with a learning disability when compared with their non-learning-disabled matched group. The experience of trauma was linked with higher rates of insecure or disorganized attachment with the child, rather than the learning disability per se.

- An attachment perspective can also be helpful in understanding potential difficulties which emerge as part of a collaborative working relationship.

Chapter 7

The Assessment Process

This chapter does not aim to act as a guide for undertaking a social work assessment; this is left to others with the relevant knowledge and experience. Rather, it aims to:

- consider the assessment process

- summarize specialist aspects of assessments conducted with parents with learning disabilities

- offer some practical ideas for use when conducting these assessments.

The assessment process

Getting the assessment process right is important because, as Wade *et al.* (2010) state, good assessments are inextricably linked with:

- effective interventions

- improved chances of successful reunification

- stable placements

- overall better outcomes for children.

The social work assessment provides the foundation; often in the case of a parent with learning disabilities, other professional assessments need to be considered, included and interpreted as well. This makes the already complex process of assessment even more challenging.

Good practice also implies that assessments are conducted in accordance with the relevant legislative context and good practice guidance. This is summarized in the HM Government's (DfE, 2015) guidance: *Working Together to Safeguard Children: A Guide to Inter-agency Working to Safeguard and Promote the Welfare of Children*. This guidance also contains a formidable appendix of useful 'further information'. However, there is little specific reference to parents with learning disabilities, so we also need to include the UN Convention on the

Rights of Persons with Disabilities, *Valuing People Now* (DH, 2009) and *Good Practice Guidance on Working with Parents with Learning Disabilities* (DH and DfE, 2007).

Within this overall guidance, direction for the structure of the assessment is contained within the *Framework for the Assessment of Children in Need and their Families* (DH, DfEE and Home Office, 2000). The Framework does not refer specifically to parents with learning disabilities as it is an overarching model, designed to be valid for all groups and remains applicable to all specialist groups. The Assessment Framework provides a structure and systematic methodology on which assessments are based rather than a step-by-step guide.

There are three domains which are all related. These are: the child's developmental needs, parenting capacity and family and environmental factors. Each domain then has a number of dimensions which help to shape and direct your assessment.

In essence, the Assessment Framework is an assessment of risk. What you are effectively doing is asking three questions:

1.   What are the parents able to do and achieve in terms of recognized parenting behaviour?

2.   What is the environmental and family context in which they operate as parents?

3.   How well does this match the developmental needs of the child?

In order to answer these questions, you will need to gain an understanding of family function, needs and capabilities, such that decisions can be made about the following (Morgan and Goff, 2004):

•   the extent of children's exposure to risk

•   the range of services needed to maintain the children in the family

•   any action required to safeguard and promote the welfare of the children in the family.

Assessment models

One of the key assessment tools will be use of in-depth interviews with family members. Smale *et al.* (2000) discuss three models to help understand and direct assessment: the *questioning*, *procedural* and *exchange models*.

In the *questioning model*, the professional takes the role of 'expert' and devises and poses questions in order to conduct the assessment. Then the information gathered is compared with research-based knowledge and theories to produce a set of conclusions. This model can be applied to any area where the professional has particular expertise, for example, in child protection, where family violence is a problem.

In the *procedural model*, the professional follows a pre-determined methodology or format to gather information. There is also a focus on standard thresholds (such as eligibility criteria), asking whether they have been met. This may be a rather inflexible approach, but can be used in conjunction with other models, and is helpful when resources are scarce.

In the *exchange model*, it is the person being assessed who is regarded as the expert; that is, he is expert on himself and his situation. The emphasis is on joint planning, with the professional working to facilitate reaching the individual's goals. This is most likely to be used when you are focussed on an assessment of needs, where the outcome is an understanding of the person's strengths, needs and resources required. An example of this might be working with a parent who has Asperger syndrome where you are asking him about special interests, sensory sensitivities and how best to present information.

Milner and O'Byrne (2009) suggest that the model or mix of models used will depend very much on the skills of individual workers and the ethos of the organization in which they practise. However, whatever the model, it must be supported by appropriate practice and research-based knowledge and, in our case, adapted for use with the client group.

Planning the assessment

The structure of the Assessment Framework, then, is only the beginning of the assessment process. It is essential to plan all assessments thoroughly, adding your professional skills. Ideally, the gathering of information should build logically to take you through the assessment and lead to meaningful conclusions. The assessment then has utility for families and involved professionals, and will stand up to the scrutiny of the court process.

At this point, useful questions to ask yourself might be:

- *What is my time schedule?* Assessments often take longer than planned, and there are several aspects to assessments undertaken with parents with learning disabilities which make them potentially time-consuming. There are a number of contributory factors, including the need to gather information from archived files or from other services (e.g., childhood medical information). If parents do not understand the importance of the assessment, they may have difficulty prioritizing your assessment visits, and interviews may need to be longer or more frequent in order to gather the information you require. If you think you will need to commission an expert report (such as an early cognitive assessment with a possible follow-up report), it is likely to take time to identify an appropriate expert with the skills you need. If the mother is pregnant, this in itself dictates the time frame; specialist assessments (such as a cognitive assessment) will have to be commissioned with this in mind. Some experts (myself included) prefer not to complete formal assessments such as IQ tests with mothers who are either heavily pregnant or have just given birth. It can be uncomfortable for mothers and variable concentration may affect results, although this differs from person to person.

- *What is the status and stability of the current family?* There are numerous variations of what constitutes the 'family' you are proposing to assess. The mother may be very young, in the early stages of a first pregnancy with an unidentified father and hostile maternal grandparents. Or the family may be just about managing to live together at home with a certain level of support from other family members. Perhaps the parents are in an on–off relationship with the children in foster care. There are many other permutations varying in complexity and predictability which will affect your assessment plan, At the same time, flexibility must be built into the plan to allow for adjustment to sudden changes: a boyfriend decides he wishes to be a 'hands-on' father, grandparents have a realistic think about their offer of support and withdraw, or an expert assessment highlights major concerns which need further exploration.

- *What are the critical pieces of information and how do I gather them?* This is about priorities, deciding what the fundamental questions are and how they will be answered. Compile a list of key questions/areas to be investigated and then consider how you will answer any questions posed with some idea of the methodology. Some of the information gathering you can manage yourself. This is probably more controllable; activities such as consulting records and conducting interviews and observations can be done in your own time frame, but they still need to be tied in to the work of others. If you need to involve other professionals, such as a health visitor, nursery nurse or a member of the community learning disabilities team, plan this in, consult with the professional and gain some commitment to your time frame. Remember: they all have their own work priorities and will not necessarily share yours!

- *How do I build a picture of the parents and their functioning?* This will be very much directed by the answers to the above questions. Information gathered can be structured by borrowing methods used in psychological risk assessments, looking at *static* and *dynamic* factors. *Static* factors are circumstances and attributes which cannot be changed. They are usually historical factors, such as an early history of abuse, but an individual's learning disability would form part of this as an existing personal attribute. *Dynamic* factors are circumstances or attributes that are open to change or fluctuate over time, such as housing, current stressors or mental health. You can see that whilst the static factors set the context, the dynamic factors, because they are fluctuating, allow the opportunity for change to be introduced.

Assessment considerations: general principles

When working with parents who have a learning disability, reports compiled by expert practitioners can be highly influential. It is critical, therefore, that assessments reflect best practice and demonstrate that the parent's learning disability has been accommodated throughout the process. It is also important to recognize that the detailed scrutiny involved as part of the assessment process, together with the implied threat of removal of the child, is highly stressful for parents. Assessments should be conducted with sensitivity and care, with a transparent and collaborative structure.

In addition, the following principles should underpin the assessment process:

- Ensure the primary focus remains on the child. Where there are people within the family who have competing significant needs (e.g. the mother has a mild learning disability and mental health needs and the father has a borderline learning disability and an early diagnosis if ADHD), it is easy for the complexity of these issues to skew priorities, with the result that the child becomes 'lost' in the process (Cleaver and Nicholson, 2007).

- Language and communication used throughout the assessment process should be accessible and understandable. Formal procedures such as assessments, child protection meetings or child care proceedings are daunting and frightening for most people; when you are unsure what is happening or what may happen next, and cannot understand explanations given, life feels even more out of control. We, the professionals who are used to working with formality and specific language (abbreviations, acronyms, medical terms, legal language), have a responsibility to tailor language and communication to meet the needs of the parent, and to work with the parent so that he feels sufficiently confident to ask for explanations (DH and DfES, 2007).

- Parents with learning disabilities will have as wide a range of support needs as any other parent. In addition, we know they are more likely to have mental health difficulties, which also may well be unrecognized and untreated; they are at increased risk of having experienced discrimination, abuse and hate crimes, and less likely to have had access to positive role models and life experiences relevant to the role of being a parent. As a consequence, parents may need prompting or help to access the wide range of supports they require.

- Research has demonstrated that, with appropriate supports and teaching, parents with learning disabilities are able to learn new skills and adapt and change their behaviour (see Chapter 8).

- We know that mothers with a learning disability are at greater risk of experiencing prenatal difficulties and are more likely to give birth prematurely and/or have babies with low birth weight (Hoglund, Lindgren and Larsson, 2012). The assessment process should begin as early as possible to ensure that support is offered during pregnancy in order to help reduce complications and establish engagement before the child is born.

- Assessments of parenting capacity should be set in context and demonstrate a consideration of external factors which have an impact on family function. We know that people with learning disabilities, including parents, are particularly vulnerable to the effects of poverty, isolation and hate crime; the changing needs of the child or children will place differing sets of demands on parents, as will the supports available (Turney et al., 2012).

- The identification of parents' functional strengths and needs, such as their individual learning style, knowledge and range of skills, gives a positive focus and indicates areas for specific, individualized support (DfE, 2015).

- Psychometric testing is usually included as part of the early assessment process in order to establish or clarify the learning disability diagnosis. This should be set within a holistic assessment which explores other individual dimensions, rather than considering cognitive abilities on their own.

- Family history should include information about previous support – not simply a list of what was provided, but an analysis of support offered, its suitability and effectiveness.

- The concept of 'good enough' parenting applies just as much to parents with learning disabilities as to the rest of the population, as do the concerns around the lack of clarity about what constitutes 'good enough' parenting. The domains and dimensions of the Assessment Framework will provide information on which a decision may be based, but interpretation of these should bear in mind the finding that the standards expected of parents with learning disabilities have been higher than those expected of other groups of parents (CSCI, 2009). Indication that evaluations reference these potential value judgements will help to demonstrate a balanced and fair assessment.

- Recommendations made should reflect an overall final aim of maintaining the child in the family, whenever possible, as laid down in guidance and legislation (UN Convention on the Rights of the Child, UN Convention on the Rights of Persons with Disabilities, Children Act 1989, Human Rights Act 1998).

- Assessments need to include the entire context of the child's learning experience. The wider community, family and friends may already be meeting some of a child's needs with resources which are routinely available. For example, a child who meets regularly with cousins of the same age living nearby will have varied play and language development opportunities; attending an Early Years nursery will provide opportunities for stimulation and learning behavioural boundaries.

Practical assessment considerations

The principles described offer a sound base for the construction of an assessment; next we consider practical considerations affecting the information-gathering process:

- Assessments should be conducted by professionals who have appropriate experience in working with adults with learning disabilities. If the lead assessor does not have this experience, then he should have the opportunity to work with a professional who does have this experience, whether an immediate colleague or a member of a specialist team such as a community learning disability nurse.

- Guidance documents (Care Act, 2014, 2015; DH, 2010b; DfE, 2015) indicate that the initial step in assessment is to consider the parents' individual support needs. These should be should be addressed first. Only then does the assessment move into an assessment of parenting capacity.

- Specific information should form part of the assessment, including the parents' current practical level of knowledge and skills, their learning strengths and difficulties and their ability to apply and use what has been learned.

- People with a learning disability are subject to social stigma and negative interpretation of their behaviour. Information gathered from some sources (e.g. 'friends' and some relatives) may be subject to distortion and should be interpreted with caution.

- Parents with learning disabilities may appear to be avoidant during the course of the assessment. However, it may be that the process of being assessed brings back unhappy and unpleasant memories of schooldays, where perhaps the experience of failure and inadequacy was uppermost. Careful explanation of what is happening and why can help to allay fears and worries.

- Parents may have a history of receiving support which did not appear to be particularly effective. The support history should be carefully evaluated, asking questions such as:

    - What was the support service?

    - Why was it provided?

    - What were the aims and goals of the support?

    - How long did it last?

    - Was it a mainstream service, or adapted for parents with a learning disability?

    - What were the overall gains over the short and long term?

    - Were there any difficulties?

- Support networks should also be carefully assessed, evaluating the contribution (and potential contribution) of both formal and informal networks of support.

- Support required should be carefully and thoroughly specified across the spectrum of parent and child needs – for example, a family member to read appointment letters, transport and housing needs, support during school holidays, skills training and social opportunities.

Specialist assessment models

Clinicians working with parents with learning disabilities have long recognized the dearth of specialized, reliable assessment material and some have gone on to develop their own material. In the UK, one of the best known and most widely used assessment formats is the Parent Assessment Manual (McGaw *et al.*, 1998). Sue McGaw developed the assessment from her parent multidimensional skills model and knowledge-skills-practice contingency (McGaw, 1997; McGaw *et al.*, 1998; McGaw and Sturmey, 1994).

The parent multidimensional skills model has a similar structure to the framework for assessment in that it has three dimensions:

1. intellectual functioning and living skills

2. family history

3. support and resources.

Each dimension has a number of domains:

- In the *intellectual functioning and living skills* domain, the focus of the dimensions is on cognitive skills, particularly problem-solving, logical sequencing and decision-making skills as well as overall intellectual functioning. Organizational abilities and practical and social functioning are also included in this category.

- In the *family history* domain, the dimensions look at life skills and learning of life skills as well as the parents' physical, mental and emotional health and nurturing experiences

- In the *support and resources* domain, the dimensions explore the support and resources available to the family: housing, transport, employment, family support and community facilities.

These three domains converge into one central area of child care.

The knowledge-skills-practice contingency emphasizes the link between parents' knowledge, their ability to use this knowledge as practical skills and their ability to use skills consistently as well as taking the principle of that skill and applying it in similar (but not the same) circumstances.

The first step (knowledge) asks what the parent knows about living independently, running a home and being a mother or father. If knowledge is limited, then we need to consider whether the parent can learn and retain the necessary information and skills.

The next question from this model is whether the parent is using this knowledge in everyday life. For example a parent may talk knowledgeably about using a 'naughty step' for discipline, but is he actually doing it? Is the parent able to make the transfer from knowledge to practical skills?

This is followed by the next step in use of skills, the rather more complex idea of being able to generalize from one learning experience to another, and using skills regularly and consistently so that they are maintained.

After developing these models, McGaw then went on to use them as the basis for the Parent Assessment Manual (PAM) and later the Parent Assessment Manual Software (PAMS) (2004) which provides an electronic parent-and-child profile.

PAM is a structured multidimensional parenting assessment which has been standardized on UK populations of parents with learning disabilities, borderline disabilities and no disabilities. There is a manual for professionals, materials – including an initial screening tool – knowledge cartoons and questionnaires about the parents' understanding of their own needs. These can be used as isolated elements or altogether for the full assessment. Again, all materials for parents are designed to be accessible and can be used as isolated elements or altogether for the full assessment.

Other assessments are available, but tend to be less widely used. McGaw and Newman (2005) give a useful summary of available functional assessments (in *What Works for Parents with Learning Disabilities*, pp.29–31). There are screening instruments available, but these tend to be fairly basic; by the time you have reached the assessment stage, a more detailed process is likely to be required. In the UK, as well as the PAM assessment, First Steps to Parenthood (Young and Strouthos, 1998) is occasionally used. This is a manual designed to be used to ascertain the parents' knowledge and help identify areas for further work, discussion or practical intervention. It contains questions in a number of relevant areas, including pregnancy and child development from 0–18 years. Assessments of this type can be useful where parents struggle to respond to more open questioning; your assessment is structured and you may find the built-in prompts of questions and topics helpful.

Remember that using a structured assessment of this type will only be worthwhile if it helps you answer questions which are relevant for the parent. And, whilst you are using the framework for assessment, it is by no means essential to use a specialist structured assessment such as the PAM. There are many other ways in which the information you need may be gathered: by observation, working alongside the parent, discussion and reflection.

An alternative method of assessing parents, particularly with respect to capacity to change, is by giving parents the opportunity to change within a managed framework. Outcomes of this 'managed' change suggest the following (Farmer *et al.*, 2008):

- The parameters for change must be defined from the start (what needs to change, when and how, levels of support and method of measurement).

- The consequences of no or insufficient change must be clearly set out and understood.

- There must be an unambiguous action plan.

- The action plan is supported by a written agreement.

- Monitoring and feedback are ongoing.

Using this methodology, Ward *et al.* (2010) found that parents of babies considered at risk of significant harm usually demonstrated an acceptable level of progress within the first six months of the child's life.

Using expert assessments

As noted, assessments of parents with learning disabilities often include or refer to other professional assessments. These are most likely to be assessments exploring the learning disability diagnosis, specialist assessments of mental health, emotional or attachment difficulties or assessments of capacity to change. The following should be noted when referring to these assessments:

- Assessors should be wary of misinterpreting historical reports. Specialist advice should be sought, particularly with respect to the effects of cognitive impairment or mental health problems in learning disability.

- Literature in the field of assessing parents with a learning disability emphasizes that cognitive abilities do not predict parenting capacity, but assessments of cognitive abilities can be helpful in determining the ways in which a person learns, remembers and uses information. These assessments should offer advice about how best to work with a parent and indicate any specific prompts or aids that are required. It is best practice to have access to this kind of information at an early stage in your assessment so that further steps are effective and appropriate.

- Expert or specialist assessments are guided by the instructions you choose to give. Before instructing another professional, think about the questions you have or the kind of advice you need, and make sure this is included in the letter of instruction.

- When using expert assessments, read them in parallel with your assessment or, if you have no written assessment, consider the expert report alongside your ideas. Draw out the observations or conclusions which are the same. Agreement helps to consolidate a point of view or decision.

- Then draw out any observations or conclusions which differ and think about why this might be. Do you need to review your ideas, investigate further, meet with the professional for a discussion or agree to differ? If you have differing ideas, review your analysis critically to ensure that your report is logical and defendable.

- Consider whether the expert has highlighted any areas that require further investigation. For example, evidence of certain attachment difficulties may suggest that the parent will have difficulty fostering a positive relationship with the child. What does this look like in practice? Have any attempts been made to support this difficulty? Is there any evidence of change?

Conclusion

At the beginning of this chapter, I commented on the importance of good assessment. The process of assessment involves the systematic collection of information, which, when working with parents who have a learning disability, must be carried out in both a sensitive and informed manner. If not, the risk is that the material collected will lack relevance and will not help to move the assessment process forward as it should.

An additional complication is that assessments of parents with a learning disability are likely to include contributions from other professionals, which must then be processed and critically analysed in order to reach a conclusion that has meaning for the child and parent. Reflection is an important part of the whole process as assumptions and expectations can be tested and considered for their validity, particularly those that relate to traditional ideas of parenting and disability. Use of a pathway based on critical analysis, knowledge drawn from experience and research balanced with a reflective process will help to ensure that assessment practices in this area are of high quality.

Summary

The main points of this chapter can be summarized as follows:

- When working with parents with learning disabilities, social work assessments often need to refer to other professional opinions, making the process particularly complex.

- The Assessment Framework provides a structure and systematic methodology but this is only the beginning of the assessment course. It is essential to plan all assessments thoroughly, adding professional skills for a meaningful process.

- The detailed scrutiny involved in assessment and the implied threat of removal of the child is highly stressful for parents. Assessments should be conducted with sensitivity and care, with a transparent and collaborative structure.

- Setting assessments in family, child, support and environmental contexts is important to give a balanced view of the demands made of parents.

- Specialist assessments may be used but only if the information gained supports the framework model and augments understanding of the child's, parents' or family's needs.

- An alternative method of assessing parents, particularly with respect to capacity to change, is by giving parents the opportunity to change within a 'managed' framework.

- Assessments conducted with parents who have a learning disability must be carried out in both a sensitive and informed manner. A pathway based on critical analysis, knowledge drawn from experience and research balanced with a reflective process will help to ensure that assessment practices in this area are of high quality.

Chapter 8

Working with Families

In this chapter, we take a practical view of working with parents who have a learning disability. This chapter:

- expands some of the points raised in Chapters 2 and 3

- looks at the use of group work and suggests adaptations which might need to be made

- considers home-based interventions

- describes competence-enhancing techniques

- discusses written and spoken communication skills, including non-verbal communication and

- defines the competencies required of practitioners.

In common with all parents, parents with learning disabilities work and learn in different ways. They bring history and experience to the process, gained:

- informally from their own parents, other family members and friends

- from helping to care for siblings or younger relatives

- from their educational experiences (school, college, work placements or work) and

- from parenting their own children (who may or may not have be in their care).

These experiences will all be applied within parents' current social context and environment.

Most parents require some kind of support with the task of being a mother or father. Often this is supplied by informal networks of family and friends, supplemented with sought information from the media or internet or community groups and primary healthcare. Some parents need additional support, perhaps because they feel ill-prepared for the role of parent, or because of specific difficulties such as caring for a child with ASD or coping with behavioural difficulties in adolescents. Often this extra support is offered in the form of parenting groups.

Groups: mainstream or specialized?

Group work with parents is a cost-effective method of service delivery, and is available in most areas, although this will not necessarily be tailored to the needs of parents with learning disabilities. A variety of parent education programmes have been developed based on two assumptions. These are:

1. Parents need particular knowledge and a range of skills and behaviours in order to care for their children successfully.

2. Following a directed course can improve these skills, knowledge and behaviours.

The Department for Education lists some 51 independently evaluated parent programmes on its website. The age range covered varies from pre-birth to adolescence, covering common issues such as child development or behaviour problems, or more specific topics such as child obesity or a diagnosis of ADHD.

In some areas, specialized parent education programmes which target the needs of a parent with a learning disability may not be readily available. A question would be whether parents are able to benefit from attending a course that is aimed at the non-learning-disabled population.

The Foundation for People with Learning Disabilities (2015) states the following principles to be followed when considering the application of a therapeutic or teaching programme for people with learning disabilities:

*   that the programme's key elements are well explained and accessible

*   that the specific needs of people with a learning disability are attended to, particularly with respect to verbal comprehension and expression, working memory, information processing and executive functioning

*   that it is recognized that additional support may be needed with a variety of issues outside the scope of the programme.

Mainstream programmes can be assessed against these factors, but even if a programme appears sufficiently accessible and supportive, the pace of participation, literacy requirements and level of thinking and understanding needed may prove difficult to manage and might even, in creating a sense of failure, have a negative effect. Some studies have shown that parents with learning disabilities benefit less from groups where participants include both learning-disabled and non-learning-disabled members, particularly when there are only a small number of people with a learning disability in the group (Booth, 2000).

However, if there are no alternatives, a programme where a few main themes are simply expressed and 'academic' demand is low may be applicable, particularly if you are able to offer additional support between sessions to emphasize or explain topics covered.

Groups: making adaptations

If appropriate material is not readily obtainable, an alternative route may be to adapt existing course material to be used in either a group setting or individually.

Glazemakers and Deboutte (2013) recognized the difficulties staff found in sourcing applicable information for working with parents with learning disabilities. They adapted the Group Triple P (positive parenting programme), taking care to use recommended adaptations that would not affect the efficacy of the programme, and investigated how well this worked with parents with learning disabilities. The Triple P programme is a well-established and evaluated set of parenting support systems, originating in Australia, but now used in many countries. The existing mainstream programme was adapted by:

- identifying the important elements of the existing programme which should be covered (continuing to include the 'key elements')

- attending to the learning needs of the group by extending the time allowed for sessions to include time for relationship building (informal chats over coffee), longer group discussion and greater emphasis on practice

- delivering sessions at a slower pace

- structuring sessions so that they would not be perceived as overwhelming

- changing the workbook writing tasks to group discussion and reflection on particular subjects instead

- providing additional support by contacting participants (by phone or visit) between sessions in order to address any issues raised and encourage attendance at the next session

- using home visits following later sessions rather than a phone call to support generalization of skills (using the techniques learned in the home or community situation)

- providing free child care during sessions

- providing additional professional support to deal with potentially disruptive issues that were not within the remit of the programme (e.g. financial concerns or partner violence).

The research concluded that the adapted group programme had positive effects on parent and child well-being, although, as this was a pilot study, they consider their results as 'preliminary'. However, it demonstrates how functional adaptation might be achieved.

Specialized groups

As the number of parents with a learning disability in the population has increased, so specialized programmes focussing on working with parents with learning disabilities has grown. Robust research on the overall effectiveness and comprehensive identification of key components is lacking, as already discussed in Chapter 2, but initial findings offer some guidance.

The general direction of research results concludes that parents with learning disabilities are able to learn, apply and maintain knowledge and skills, with behavioural teaching methods seeming to be most effective (IASSID, 2008). Workers in the field are beginning to apply more holistic and rounded methods, but these have not yet been the subject of sound evaluation. McGaw and Newman (2005) indicate inclusion of both behavioural methods:

- building on parents' existing skills and knowledge rather than focussing on difficulties

- using modelling, feedback and social rewards (praise)

- using tangible rewards under some circumstances (e.g. to encourage attendance)

- providing teaching in the environment in which those skills will be used

and inclusion of holistic factors:

- focussing on securing positive engagement over the long term

- incorporating elements which actively promote child resilience

- recognizing the importance of family, culture and environment

- promoting social inclusion

- continuing teaching long-term, offering different interventions at different stages of child development.

Rather than directly focussing on teaching skills, some groups may be offered in order to provide general support. Parents with learning disabilities themselves have reported experiencing increased confidence and levels of self-esteem as a result of attending social support groups (Booth and Booth, 2003), although this does not necessarily have a direct effect on parenting skills.

Home-based interventions

As research highlights that home-based, skills-focussed, individualized and behaviourally oriented programmes are the most likely to yield positive results (Feldman, 2010), one-to-one work in the family home would seem to provide the optimum location. Strengths of work within the home are:

- Teaching can be completely individualized, allowing the parent to work in partnership with the professional.

- Teaching is specific in each home context so that skills can be both taught and practised with as few obstacles as possible.

- Attendance and child care is less of an issue.

- If one partner works, times can be flexibly negotiated to include both parents.

But the home situation brings potential problems as well:

- Homes contain many distractions: the needs of any children who are at home, neighbours and friends calling in, television, preoccupation with social media. Any successful work has to identify these distractions and either eliminate them (routinely turning the TV off) or incorporate them in the teaching (involving children in a housework or shopping task).

- Immediate and pressing personal difficulties may have to be dealt with before any formal work can begin. It is helpful to recognize this eventuality and (like some group programmes) set aside time to discuss these issues.

- If the parent has only limited control over the home environment, work may be undermined by an uncooperative partner or relative. In this situation, influential others should be identified and included in the work undertaken, or their behaviour actively managed (McGaw and Newman, 2005).

- This method requires staff time in terms of travel and visits; it is helpful to secure management backing for an intervention (suddenly ceasing work without preparation could be damaging) and to record progress carefully, so that results are demonstrable.

Feldman (2010) describes a parent teaching home visit as typically lasting from one to two hours. This begins by revisiting what was covered in the previous visit and looking at whether the parent has been able to use these new skills. In order to ensure that learning is maintained, the parent then demonstrates these skills, followed by feedback and praise. The next step is to work on the current task, making sure that only one or two components are tackled at a time. Training is given (see 'Competence-enhancing techniques' below), again with feedback and plenty of praise as a social reward. Once this formal section of the visit has been completed, then time is available for other personal issues to be discussed.

We will now take a more detailed look at the teaching element of these visits, with an emphasis on behavioural teaching methods, their use in errorless learning and a consideration of the memory component in learning.

Competence-enhancing techniques

Before any teaching can start, there are some essential early stages which must be completed. First, there must be good rapport between the professionals involved and the family. Establishing rapport is helped when parents are able to see that what you are trying to achieve:

- is relevant for them
- will contribute positively to parents' care of their children
- does not seek to patronize.

You can enhance rapport by:

- asking the parents for help and attending to their views and ideas
- empowering parents, encouraging them to say when they do not like or want something
- promoting spontaneous questioning from parents
- working in an open and honest manner
- taking a holistic view of the family's needs
- not using negative body language and facial expressions
- not talking about parents in front of them or talking over them

- leaving time for a response to your questions

- not adopting a parent–child style of interaction (where you are the parent).

Collaborative assessment and working methods between professionals and the family are the best way to accomplish these objectives; positive relationships will build as the parent begins to feel she is making progress.

The next stage is an assessment of where the parent is with respect to strengths and areas of need (dealt with in more detail in Chapter 7). This will effectively define areas of teaching to be covered. All parents will have a partial set of skills and possibly some unhelpful or inaccurate knowledge and behaviours requiring change. When you are working with two parents, separate sets of goals should be developed for each, within a complementary overall plan. Behaviourally based working methods are supported by research; these teaching methods have long been recognized as effective in working with people who have a range of learning needs. For more information detailed in this area, I would suggest reference to such basic texts as: Miltenberger (2007) *Behaviour Modification: Principles and Procedures*; Szidon and Franzone (2009) *Task Analysis*; or Willis, LaVigna, and Donnellan (1993) *Behavior Assessment Guide*. A brief introduction to basic behavioural techniques follows.

GOALS

A completed assessment will enable you to give initial feedback to the parent about likely goals, listen to the parents' ideas and agree an appropriately paced joint learning schedule. Develop clear and accurate goals so that parents understand what is expected of them and are able to recognize their achievements. For example, 'Julie will read to Owen more and show him affection' is not a clear goal. Instead the following gives the necessary detail: 'Between 6.30 and 7.00pm each night, Julie will say to Owen, "Time for a cuddle and book", and will sit on the sofa with the TV off. They will read one of his books (already sorted and placed in a special box) for ten minutes and tick the chart to say they have done this together.' Remember the 'who, what, when, where, how' of behaviour and include how you will monitor progress. In my clinical experience, it is often the monitoring which is forgotten, but this makes it difficult to know what is happening in your absence. Try to make recording as simple and effective as possible, make sure you refer to this recording during formal sessions (to emphasize its importance) and use it as a basis for positive feedback and praise. Goals must be achievable and meaningful for parents and should be changed only when achieved. If a parent is not achieving goals, you may have made it too difficult and should try cutting the task down further using task analysis.

TASK ANALYSIS

This involves breaking a task down into its component parts. There is no right or wrong way to do this, which allows you to tailor steps to the learning patterns of any parent. The parent can tell you what she thinks she is able to manage, making this a joint effort. A typical task analysis will:

- Identify an end goal.

- Identify the cue – when you do the task. This may not always be relevant, but, for example, when teaching potty training, the cue might be 'after Jon has had a drink'.

- Identify the main components of the task, in logical order. If you find this hard, watch someone do the task and write down the main steps.

- Think about any skills a parent may need to have before beginning (e.g. when filling bottles, can the parent recognize numbers or do you have to get round this by using a sticker to indicate levels?).

- Decide how the task will be taught (whole task, forward or backward chaining). To decide this, think about how the parent has learned successfully in the past, her temperament and where she will need to use the task.

- Decide on presentation – will the steps be written out, pictures used, demonstration or a combination?

- State how you record progress.

- State when to move on to another task (i.e. clarify what success looks like). Do you need the parent to be right all the time (as in making up bottles) or just right most of the time (as in learning potty training)?

The advantage of this technique is that it focusses attention on the key parts of any task, which helps learning and retention. It also spells out one agreed method for everybody to use. This is important as parents are easily confused when professionals recommend varying ways of completing the same task.

CHAINING

Once a task has been broken down into actions, and the steps put in sequence, the task is taught one step at a time. It may suit the parent better, and give a greater sense of achievement, if steps are taught in a short sequence, with prompts used to ensure success. Backward chaining is a useful idea – you begin with the final step of the task first (success in itself) and work backwards through the steps until the parent is completing the whole task from start to end. So, with the task of bathing a baby, forward chaining would begin with assembling all the equipment, then filling the bath, checking temperature, undressing the baby and so on, whereas backward chaining would start with you completing most of the task, but offering the final step of drying and dressing the bathed baby to the parent, and then working backwards from there. The method you choose and the size of steps depends very much on individual progress, but can be adjusted as you go along.

PROMPTING

By prompting, you are helping the parent along with unfamiliar routines and jobs as she learns new skills. Prompts may be:

- gestural, showing what to do

- verbal (e.g. hints – 'what's next?', suggestions – 'try opening the cupboard', or directions – 'now you wrap him in the towel')

- visual (e.g. notes, pictures, objects)

- model (going through the next step alongside the parent)

- physical (sometimes a full prompt where you guide someone's arm or give a nudge); this kind of prompting requires care and an agreement with the parent that it is OK.

Prompts need to be faded out at some point usually as the parent's skill grows, prompts are needed less and less. Some prompting methods such as pictorial reminders can be left in place (taped to the wall or fridge) for as long as required.

REWARDS

Use of rewards, or positive reinforcement, is a fundamental part of teaching new skills and increasing positive behaviours. It also presents a good model; if parents feel the positive benefits of praise, they are more likely to incorporate this into their behaviour as a parent. What we are doing with rewards is saying 'yes, that's right', but also marking an achievement and making that behaviour more likely to happen in the future. Rewards are usually:

- Social – the easiest to use as you can smile and offer praise at any time. When using social praise as a reward, remember positive body language is important and that your praise must be noticeable and evident. A quick 'good' muttered quietly is probably not very rewarding, and although you might feel a little silly exaggerating your delight, this may be exactly what is needed. Encouraging self-praise (or partners praising each other) is a helpful way of fading out your role as the giver of social rewards. Ask parents to notice their own achievements and be proud of what they have done.

- Tangible – these are either objects or activities. Normally, objects would be less likely to be used, but you might offer an activity, such as going out for a coffee, at particular points in your work. The novelty of objects or activities may wear off quite quickly, so use these types of reward sparingly.

- Natural – these are the ordinary results of the behaviour. They are useful to highlight as they will continue to occur; for example, playing with a baby, you could point out 'look at how he giggles and enjoys it'.

Some parents are not used to being praised; you may have to begin with quieter but genuine praise whilst the parent learns to accept her value and attainment.

ERRORLESS LEARNING

Learning usually takes place by a method of trial and error. That is, you try to complete a task and your behaviour is shaped by the reward of getting it right (or the consequences of getting it wrong). This is an effective learning method for people who:

- are confident learners

- will gather information to make a calculated good attempt

- will remember their thought processes and actions

- will use feedback constructively.

This is unlikely to be the most helpful strategy for people with learning disabilities to use. Errorless learning is a teaching process which is designed so that mistakes are not made as the learning progresses. Fish *et al.* (2015) state that it is more effective for people who:

- are anxious or lacking in confidence

- have difficulty learning new things and often get things wrong

- do not necessarily use feedback to change their behaviour

- have difficulty remembering what they have done

- have memory problems generally.

Making many errors and feeling anxious will both increase mistakes and decrease motivation, so it makes sense to avoid this. It also seems that mistakes are more likely to be remembered, either because of the emotion associated with being wrong or because the mistake is a new, self-generated behaviour and self-generated behaviours are more likely to be recalled. So, what is errorless learning?

Errorless learning harnesses behavioural principles in such a way as to avoid negative learning. You:

- construct the task so that the correct action is more or less certain to follow

- demonstrate or explain what is expected until this is very clearly understood

- use task analysis to break things down

- use prompting or collaborative working to get round difficult parts

- keep giving prompts as needed

- jump in with a prompt if you see a problem about to occur

- repeat many times to ensure retention.

In order to be successful, errorless learning depends very much on the ability of the trainer to observe and respond to the needs of the trainee; it takes practice to master an effective teaching technique.

MEMORY

Difficulties with taking in, holding on to and recall of information are usually associated with learning disabilities. Any work undertaken with parents, in order to have longevity, must have built-in strategies to support remembering. Some strategies that can be easily used jointly with families are as follows:

- Have regular routines in place. Once they are learned and familiar, this will help structure days or activities: all members of the family will find the predictability helpful.

- Organize. Store linked items together (e.g. bathing equipment) and encourage the habit of putting things away in the right place.

- Plan ahead – whether just going out for the day or what the family is going to do during half-term. You may have to lead on this initially to demonstrate the process.

- Use a diary or calendar to track appointments and important dates. This can be pictorial, use single letters to denote different visits or be more detailed, depending on literacy skills.

- Use lists, but don't get too complicated; one list at a time is best. As with calendars, these can be as simple or detailed as needed.

- Highlighter pens can be useful with lists and calendars to emphasize really important things.

- Focus on one thing at a time.

- Be prepared to repeat teaching, advice or activities many times. Using a spoken commentary (where the parent makes her own commentary) may aid retention.

- Be consistent about what you teach and how you teach it. Make sure others in the support circle (professionals, family and friends) support this consistency.

- Personalize teaching to the parent or family. Relevant information or material will be more engaging.

- Remember that high levels of stress and poor sleep will interfere with learning generally and memory in particular. Try to create a calm and positive learning environment.

- Distractions will also have a negative effect on memory; minimize interruptions and disturbances by, for example, prior agreement to switch off mobile phones for the course of the teaching.

- Giving too much information to remember increases stress and anxiety and will be counterproductive. Pace memory expectations carefully, with the parent's memory span in mind.

- Introducing several high-demand tasks in a session is likely to result in less learning as early information is forgotten. Work on one task, area or subject at a time.

It is important to remember that competence-enhancing programmes of this kind are not the complete solution, as parents and families are likely to require a range of supports from different sources. Aunos, Feldman and Goupil (2008), for example, describe a programme of support, adapted from an original programme aimed at families living in poverty in the US. This contains both child and parent elements in a flexible two-generation agenda. The child component could contain parent education on development and stimulation, with joint work with the school or pre-school and health and safety monitoring by child health. The parent or family factor could include financial advice, advocacy, specialized psychological counselling and support to establish longer-term community networks.

In the UK, Tarleton, Ward and Howarth (2007) give a list of up to 17 possible sources of support from courses and groups, counselling and advocacy to short breaks services and support with children's academic development. This demonstrates the possible complexity of support programmes. Establishing and maintaining practicable support packages forms part of the everyday work of the children and family social worker and other professionals in the field. For such packages to be successful, it is essential that there is good collaborative working and communication between the different systems, including statutory, voluntary, community and family systems.

Communication

Fundamental to high-quality support for parents with learning disabilities is that all communication involved is both clear and effective. This applies to both written and spoken communications, which should be specifically tailored to the needs of parents with learning disabilities.

Written information

Recognizing the need for people with learning disabilities to be able to have access to good-quality information at critical points in their lives (including on becoming a parent), the Department of Health issued the guidance *Making Written Information Easier to Understand for People with Learning Disabilities* (DH, 2010a). This guidance aims to create a consistency in information produced by statutory bodies for people with learning disabilities. It builds on the Disability Rights Commission's guidelines *Easy Read: How to Use Easy Words and Pictures* (Disability Rights Commission 2006) but emphasizes that guidelines should be applied flexibly and used in conjunction with existing good practice.

Before beginning to create any information, it is worth taking a little time to prepare. First, think about why you are producing the information, what you want to communicate and who your audience is. For example, the information may be about a specific activity (i.e. for just one parent) or to be used at a shared meeting with a group of parents.

Then think about the communication needs of the people who will be using the information. If you don't know what these are, then make an effort to find out, either as part of prior assessment(s) or by discussing with the individuals concerned what sort of presentation they find most helpful.

It is also useful to think about how the information will be used – is it for one use (e.g. a meeting agenda), or is it to keep and refer to over time?

Finally, consider what is the most appropriate format to use.

FORMATS

The document *Accessible Communication Formats* (DWP and ODI, 2014) reminds us that if documents are written simply, using plain English and direct explanation with no jargon terms, they will already be more accessible to a large group of people. So perhaps the first step in accessible communication is to develop the habit of clear communication.

Written formats may be used, but care must be taken about how the document is presented and the language used. More information on preparing a document can be found later in this chapter.

Easy Read is a particular written format, created to help people with learning disabilities understand information easily. In Easy Read, pictures are used to help explain the meaning. It aims to give key pieces of information without confusing background information. For this reason, many people choose to read Easy Read summaries of long documents; it can also be a helpful format for people who do not speak English fluently. More information can be found in the document *Making Written Information Easier to Understand for People with Learning Disabilities* (DH, 2010a).

CDs are a format that can be used independently – without a support worker to help explain. They can be used alongside printed information or on their own. As an audio aid, CDs have limitations in terms of explaining actions, but may be helpful as an alternative way of presenting long documents.

Video and DVD are familiar visual media which may be used together with or instead of written documents. Videos and DVDs are versatile; they can be used for informing, observing and giving feedback, and may be a more appealing method of passing on information. Videos or DVDs should be about 30 minutes long or less. If the subject is complicated, a series of short videos or DVDs is better than one lengthy piece.

DVDs and videos can be a better format for teaching skills such as feeding your baby. They may be used in sessions and at home.

Mobile phones and tablets have a variety of functions depending on the model and contract. They can be used as a basic diary, for reminders, short videos and quick access to information (with internet availability). However, these will only function when in working order and fully charged!

Producing written information

Summarizing advice from *Making Written Information Easier to Understand for People with Learning Disabilities* (DH, 2010a), *Accessible Communication Formats* (DWP and ODI, 2014) and other sources, the following steps are recommended:

TEXT

- Use a large font size (at least 14), with a clear font (e.g. Arial, sans serif or a similar plain font).

- Leave extra space between lines, at least 1.3 spacing.

- Break up text and highlight important points – for example, using bullet points.

- Colour may be used to indicate separate topics.

- Use bold, not italics, to emphasize points.

- Limit your use of capital letters; don't use capital block headings (the words lack a familiar shape and will be harder to read).

- Start new topics on a fresh page.

- Usually, you need good contrast between paper and print – for example, black print on matt cream or pastel paper. Sometimes people with specific difficulties require less glare and have particular needs (see Chapter 3 on dyslexia).

PICTURES

- Pictures are used to help explain the written information, with one picture per idea. Make sure that the image used clarifies the text and gives an accurate meaning of what the text is about.

- Too many illustrations are confusing.

- Pictures are usually positioned to the left of the text.

- Drawings, photographs or other images may be used. Cartoon images are sometimes less easily understood. If in doubt, test on your users.

- Only use one style of picture throughout.

- Use large and clear images, in colour if possible.

- Don't use symbols or abstract graphics.

WORDS

- Use simple words and language.

- Avoid jargon, acronyms and abbreviations.

- Explain difficult words if they must be used.

- You can put a glossary at the back of the document which acts as a reminder of complex words.

- Use natural language rather than following strict grammatical rules.

- Keep sentences short – less than 15 words.

- Use full stops and commas, but avoid lots of punctuation, such as semi-colons and colons.

- Use full words (do not) rather than a contraction (don't); some people need to read the 'not' to understand the meaning.

- Don't worry about repetition. It is better to use the same words when describing the same thing.

- Use written numbers rather than figures.

- Try not to use percentages; instead, explain, such as half or one out of every two people.

- For time, avoid the 24-hour clock. Pictures of a clock showing the time may help.

Spoken communication

When talking to parents, the same basic principles of simplicity and clarity remain central. Many people with a learning disability would rather gloss over not understanding than halt a conversation and ask for clarification. Many have a background of failure with respect to learning new skills. Make sure that you are not recreating a classroom environment and bringing back bad memories of lack of school success. If you are able to communicate effectively with parents, the quality of relationships between you and the family will be greatly enhanced. It is important to create a communication climate where the parent can say 'I don't get it' or 'I don't understand'. You need to acknowledge that the tasks you are tackling together are complicated and sometimes difficult to explain – for example, 'This is hard to explain, please say if I don't explain it properly' or 'Let me say that again and I will try to be clear'. You also need to check that the person you are talking to has understood, by asking her to summarize key points. Non-verbal communication is important and will convey information about mood, attitude and motivation. Observe non-verbal behaviour, and incorporate any information gained into your conversation. For example, 'I can see you are looking very anxious about this. How can we talk about this so you are not so worried?' Or you could change topics or take a different angle on the subject under discussion. In general, in your communication aim to:

- use simple vocabulary and plain English with no jargon

- take things slowly

- speak in short sentences

- plan what you want to say

- concentrate on facts, statements or clear instructions

- use natural gestures to illustrate what you are saying

- use words or phrases in a literal way

- not interrupt

- check back that she has correctly understood

- allow people plenty of time to think and then time to speak (often longer than you might think; it takes time to process information and produce a response)

- ask one simple question at a time

- expand yes or no answers from the parent, to make sure you both understand what is being said

- talk about things in the here and now (time concepts may be difficult – future, past)

- use concrete, everyday terms rather than abstract concepts (e.g. if time is a difficult concept, use an idea which has meaning for the person, such as 'after breakfast' or 'when you go shopping')

- minimize distractions

- allow time for breaks to help concentration

- repeat the important messages.

Non-verbal communication

Our non-verbal behaviour forms an important part of communication and is particularly important when working with people with learning disabilities as they may rely on non-verbal cues to help interpret the spoken word. As establishing engagement and maintaining rapport are such important components of work with parents, it is helpful to monitor your non-verbal behaviour and make sure that it is giving a consistent message. Thinking about the non-verbal communication of the parents as well will help you understand their unspoken messages and aid the engagement process.

FACIAL EXPRESSION

Someone's facial expression is something we notice straightaway and react to quickly. Smiles, frowns or anxious looks convey strong messages which should act as cues for you to continue or modify what you are doing or saying. Non-verbal behaviours show large variation between cultures, but emotion-related facial expressions (sad, happy, angry, frightened) tend to be similar.

GESTURE
These include deliberate movements and signals (waving, pointing, beckoning). Gestures are more likely to be related to culture, so check on any cultural misunderstandings which may arise so that you can avoid them.

PARALINGUISTICS
This category includes tone of voice, pitch, volume and inflection. Generally, enthusiasm and approval is inferred from a firm, bright, moderately pitched voice, whereas a quiet, hesitant, low tone suggests you may not be sure of what you are doing, resulting in a lack of confidence in the listener. Try to be aware of your vocal tone, and match it to the emotion you are trying to convey.

POSTURE
Non-verbal postures such as sitting with arms crossed have been rather simplistically interpreted by popular media as 'defensive' – it is rather more subtle and complex than this suggests. Nevertheless, feelings and attitudes are powerfully conveyed by body posture; remembering to use a neutral, relaxed, open position will help emphasize a readiness to listen.

The space around us we see as 'ours' is referred to as personal space. This is an important but variable factor in non-verbal communication. Variability depends on culture, familiarity, the situation and personal characteristics. In our society, normal conversational distance is between about 50 and 125 centimetres (18 inches to four feet), but if someone is anxious, angry or upset, this is likely to increase.

EYE CONTACT
Normal, steady eye contact aids the exchange of emotional as well as verbal information. Parents may have particular difficulties with eye contact due to specific conditions, such as ASD (see Chapter 5). Mental health difficulties (depression, anxiety) and emotional problems such as very low self-esteem may also be associated with difficulties in maintaining usual levels of eye contact. It can help to position yourself to the side of the person you are talking to, rather than directly opposite. This relieves the burden of expected eye contact and helps both parties to feel more relaxed about talking.

TOUCH
We convey many emotions through the medium of touch, from messages about our status and power to sympathy, love and agreement. However, in a professional relationship touch is not actively used as it is a strong medium of communication and may be misinterpreted. Some parents you may be working with will have experienced emotionally damaging forms of touch and, as a result, have internalized skewed ideas of what touch means. It is advisable to

self-monitor your personal use of touch as a communication and be highly aware of your behaviour as a professional.

Non-verbal communication is, like all forms of communication, a two-way process. You must think about your own non-verbal behaviour as well as that of the parent you are working with. Developing the habit of thinking about what you do as well as what you say will help not only relationships with parents in the context of this book, but professional relationships generally. When working directly with parents, avoid focussing on one particular non-verbal behaviour and thinking 'because x does this, it means this'. It is more helpful to consider behaviours in groups – that is, the verbal communication along with her eye contact, posture and expression – to think about the overall message. To find out more about this area, a good overall reference with more detail on non-verbal communication is *Interpersonal Communication: Everyday Encounters* (Wood, 2010).

Practitioner skills and competencies

This chapter illustrates the range of skills and knowledge that are required in order to work successfully with parents with learning disabilities. These are now reviewed and summarized.

Limited attention is paid in the literature to the question of who should be undertaking specific work with parents, and whether specific qualifications are necessary.

Gates (2010) analysed the conclusions of a focus group of people with learning disabilities who were considering the question of the general attributes of supportive professionals. They identified trustworthiness, positive attitudes and a pleasant personality (someone to get along with) as important personal factors. They highlighted the need for professionals to have a good understanding of learning disabilities, so that their particular difficulties would be easily understood and processes adjusted accordingly.

Traustadottir and Sigurjonsdottir (2010) emphasize the importance of professionals who are supporting parents with learning disabilities having positive and empowering attitudes towards people with learning disabilities. They also comment on the need for sensitive management of power imbalances within client-professional relationships.

Feldman (2010) offers a number of suggestions for specific areas of competence:

Knowledge and skills:

- working with adults with learning disabilities
- child care and development

- building rapport
- behavioural teaching skills and knowledge
- observation skills.

Personal qualities and attitudes:

- empathic and sensitive
- without preconceptions
- competence inhibiting.

Supporting Parents with Learning Disabilities and Difficulties: Stories of Positive Practice (Norah Fry Research Centre, 2009) highlights the importance of:

- working in partnership with other agencies
- a flexible approach to working methods
- a proactive stance towards intervention
- working within a supporting parents model rather than a child protection model (although this will depend on circumstances).

The consensus is that a combination of enabling attitudes and positive personal qualities, with the addition of knowledge of adult learning disability, child development and basic behavioural techniques are necessary attributes of professionals working in this area. The message for recruitment and training is that selection of an individual with positive personal attributes can be supplemented by targeted training and mentoring in order to enhance the workforce.

Summary

The main points of this chapter can be summarized as follows:

- Mainstream parenting programmes can be assessed for suitability with respect to the accessibility of information, the learning needs required and the availability of additional support. However, apparent suitability should be balanced against the risk of the negative effects of creating a sense of failure.

- Functional adaptation of existing mainstream parenting programmes is achievable.

- The general direction of research results concludes that specialized groups using behavioural teaching methods seem to an effective way of working with parents with learning disabilities. More holistic and rounded methods are beginning to be explored, but these have not yet been the subject of sound evaluation.

- One-to-one behaviourally based work which takes place in the family home appears to offer the greatest opportunities in terms of personalizing content and approach.

- Establishing and enhancing rapport with parents are important first steps, followed by collaborative assessment and working methods which are rooted in behavioural theory.

- Specific adaptation to written material is needed, and attention to spoken and non-verbal communication will support positive progress with parents.

- Practitioners should have a range of relevant skills and knowledge, positive attitudes, personal qualities and working practices.

Chapter 9

Conclusions

The debate about what constitutes 'good enough' parenting is a central issue for discussion in all parenting assessments. It is especially important for parents with a learning disability when we consider that they are more likely to be subject to close scrutiny, that parents are frightened that their children may be 'taken away' and won't necessarily understand the child protection or care proceedings processes they may find themselves a part of.

There are no specific and agreed definitions of parental competence; the idea of parental competence is viewed as a continuum, with abusive and neglectful parenting leading to death at one extreme and positive parenting at the other. Interim terms have been suggested, such as adequate parenting, minimal parenting competence and 'good enough' care; defining these descriptors has proven much more difficult. With these shifting standards, if assessing the competence of any parent is difficult, the assessment of parents with particular needs, including parents who have borderline or mild learning disabilities, possibly co-ocurring with mental health problems or ASD, is much more complex.

Some parents, because of fears associated with child removal, may seek to hide their disability; this prevents adjustment and support being introduced at an early stage. Other parents will not have their learning disability (and other associated difficulties) diagnosed early enough, and support that is provided is inadequate or inappropriate.

Although we must recognize that having a learning disability will impact on parenting, focussing solely on the learning disability as the source of problems, with the implication that this is unchangeable, is poor practice. Instead, parents must be understood with reference to family, social, community and cultural perspectives, and the multiple influences on parents' beliefs, values and attitudes explored.

The differing cultures of the services likely to be involved in working with parents who have learning disabilities can cause added and unnecessary friction. In child protection, the safety of the child is the primary concern, with independence a factor; if parents are unable to care for a child independently, then their capability should be questioned. In disability cultures, the primary concern is working with the individual to achieve his maximum potential, with the requirement for support assumed. Although it is possible to work towards achieving both goals, at some point they may clash, at which time a third culture of the adversarial court process is added.

Rates of removal of children from parents with learning disabilities have remained much the same over the 1990s and early twenty-first century and concerns around the sensitivity of the process remain high.

Anti-discrimination laws have resulted in guidance and a greater awareness of the requirement to improve services for parents with learning disabilities. The involvement of user groups has helped to strengthen this process. However, public services have been under stress from the drive to cut spending; at national policy levels, it must be a priority to support local services with adequate and protected funding in order to ensure that the rhetoric of government policies can be followed up in practice.

Research has a key part to play in supporting best practice in this area. The emphasis has moved from looking at whether parent training models for parents with learning disabilities can be effective, through to expansion of these models to include assessment components. Current research is beginning to take a more contextual approach and includes evaluations of personal experience and attitudes as well as a wider exploration of risk reduction by beginning to identify factors that promote positive child development and mitigate problems in families where one or both parents have a learning disability.

Although progress continues at a macro level, it is still possible for individual professionals to adapt their practice in such a way to improve (even in small ways) the work they are doing. This book aims to help the process of enhancing individual practice and the main themes can be summarized as follows:

- If we accept that having a learning disability will impact on parenting, the overall effect will interact with the person's individual context and this should be a focus of assessments and support.

- Although tests of cognitive functioning and IQ scores give some idea of cognitive capacity and are helpful in understanding a person's presentation, this is only part of the overall picture. They do not describe emotional, social and environmental functioning, all of which must be considered in the same way as they would with all parents.

- In addition, attention should be paid to specific vulnerabilities associated with having a learning disability, such as social isolation, exploitation by powerful others and economic vulnerability.

- Early involvement, including accurate assessment, the timely provision of support and use of monitoring and feedback as part of a positive intervention may help to reduce the over-representation of parents with intellectual disability in the child protection system.

- Research has its part to play in supporting professional practice by providing relevant evidence-based information which is rooted in everyday practice.

- Despite different thresholds for services which hinder collaboration, fostering local relationships between professionals will help joint working at a 'grass roots' level.

Resources

General
Am I making myself clear?
www.accessibleinfo.co.uk/pdfs/Making-Myself-Clear.pdf

Barnardos
www.barnardos.org.uk

Best Beginnings
www.bild.org.uk/information/relationships

British Institute of Learning Disabilities (BILD)
www.bild.org.uk/information/relationships

The BILD website has a number of relevant publications and links. They will also try to help with specific queries. The link above provides access to easy-read leaflets on relationships, marriage, maternity, parenting and helping people with learning disabilities to speak for themselves.

CHANGE 'People with learning disabilities working for equal rights'
www.changepeople.co.uk

BOOKLETS

You and Your Baby 0–1

You and Your Little Child 1–5

My Pregnancy, My Choice

There is also guidance on making information accessible.

Family Action
www.family-action.org.uk/section.aspx?id=782

Good Practice Guidance on Working with Parents with a Learning Disability
www.bris.ac.uk/sps/wtpn/policyessentials/index.html

Inclusive support for parents with a learning disability
http://socialwelfare.bl.uk/subject-areas/services-client-groups/adults-disabilities/mencap/1487552011_inclusive_support_for_parents.pdf

Norah Fry Research Centre
www.bristol.ac.uk/norahfry

RNIB
www.rnib.org.uk/seeitright
Guidelines for producing information for visually impaired people.

Scottish Consortium for Learning Disabilities
http://www.enable.org.uk/families/Documents/Good%20Practice%20Guidelines%20for%20Supporting%20Parents%20with%20Learning%20Disabilities.pdf

Think Family Toolkit
http://webarchive.nationalarchives.gov.uk/20130401151715/http://www.education.gov.uk/publications/eOrderingDownload/Think-Family.pdf
Co-ordinating services for families with additional needs.

Working Together with Parents Network (WTPN)
www.bristol.ac.uk/sps/wtpn

Assessment resources
McGaw, S. (2007) *Parent Assessment Manual* (2nd edn). Truro: Pill Creek Publishing. www.pillcreekpublishing.com/pams_more.html
Morgan, P. and Goff, A. (2004) *Learning Curves: The Assessment of Parents with a Learning Disability. A Manual for Practitioners*. Norfolk Safeguarding Children Board. www.nscb.norfolk.gov.uk/documents/learningCurves.pdf
Young, S. and Strouthos, M. (1998) *First Steps to Parenthood*. Brighton: Pavilion.

References

Alexander, R. and Cooray, S. (2003) 'Diagnosis of personality disorders in learning disability.' *British Journal of Psychiatry 182*, 44, 28–31.

APA (American Psychiatric Association) (2013) *Diagnostic and Statistical Manual of Mental Health Disorders, 5th edition.* Washington and London: American Psychiatric Publishing.

Attwood, T. (1999) *Asperger's Syndrome: A Guide for Parents and Professionals.* London: Jessica Kingsley Publishers.

Aunos, M., Feldman, M. and Goupil, G. (2008) 'Mothering with intellectual disabilities: relationships between social support, health and well-being, parenting and child behaviour outcomes.' *Journal of Applied Research in Intellectual Disabilities 21*, 320–330.

Aunos, M., Goupil, G. and Feldman, M.A. (2004) 'Mothers with an intellectual disability who do and do not have custody of their children.' *Journal on Developmental Disabilities 10*, 65–79.

Bagner, D.M., Pettit, J.W., Lewinsohn, P.M. and Seeley, J.R. (2010) 'Effect of maternal depression on child behavior: a sensitive period?' *Journal of the American Academy of Child Adolescent Psychiatry 49*, 699–707.

Baker, J.K., Fenning, R.M., Crnic, K.A., Baker, B.L. and Blacher, J. (2007) 'Prediction of skills in 6-year-old children with and without developmental, delays: contributions of early regulation and maternal scaffolding.' *American Journal on Mental Retardation 112*, 375–391.

Banks, R. (2003) 'Psychological treatments for people with learning disabilities.' *Psychiatry 2*, 9, 62–64.

Baron-Cohen, S., Wheelwright, S., Robinson, J. *et al.* (2005) 'The Adult Asperger Assessment (AAA): a diagnostic method.' *Journal of Autism and Developmental Disorders 35*, 807–819.

Bartholomew, K. and Horowitz, L.M. (1991) 'Attachment styles among young adults: a test of a four-category model.' *Journal of Personality and Social Psychology 61*, 2, 226–244.

Baum, S., Gray, G. and Stevens, S. (2011) *Good Practice Guidance for Clinical Psychologists when Assessing Parents with Learning Disabilities.* Leicester: British Psychological Society.

Baurain, C. and Nader-Grosbois, N. (2013) 'Theory of mind, socio-emotional problem-solving, socio-emotional regulation in children with intellectual disability and in typically developing children.' *Journal of Autism and Developmental Disorders 43*, 5 1080–1098.

Baxter, A.J., Brugha, T.S., Erskine, H.E., Scheurer, R.W., Vos, T. and Scott, J.G. (2015) 'The epidemiology and global burden of autism spectrum disorders.' *Psychological Medicine 45*, 3, 601–613.

Behar, R. (2004) 'Alcohol consumption and eating disorders: evidence, similarities and implications.' *Revista Chilena de Neuro-Psiquiatria 42*, 3, 183–194.

Bernier, A. and Meins, E. (2008) 'A threshold approach to understanding the origins of attachment disorganization.' *Developmental Psychology 44*, 969–982.

Biederman, J., Klein, R.G., Pine, D.S. and Klein, D.F. (1998) 'Resolved: mania is mistaken for ADHD in prepubertal children.' *Journal of the American Academy of Child & Adolescent Psychiatry 37*, 1091–1093.

Bonner, A. (2006) *Social Exclusion and the Way Out: An Individual and Community Response to Human Social Dysfunction.* Chichester: Wiley and Sons.

Booth, T. (2000) 'Parents with learning difficulties, child protection and the courts.' *Representing Children 13*, 3, 175–188.

Booth, T. and Booth, W. (1998) *Growing up with Parents Who Have Learning Difficulties.* London: Routledge.

Booth, T. and Booth, W. (2003) 'Self-advocacy and supported learning for mothers with learning difficulties.' *Journal of Learning Disabilities 7*, 2, 165–193.

Booth, T., Booth, W. and McConnell, D. (2005) 'Care proceedings and parents with learning difficulties: comparative prevalence and outcomes in an English and Australian court sample.' *Child and Family Social Work 10*, 353–360.

Bordin, E.S. (1979) 'The generalizability of the psychoanalytic concept of the working alliance.' *Psychotherapy Theory, Research & Practice 16*, 252–269.

Bowlby, J. (1969) *Attachment and Loss*. New York: Basic Books.

Breslau, N., Lucia, V.C. and Alvarado, G.F. (2006) 'Intelligence and other predisposing factors in exposure to trauma and posttraumatic stress disorder.' *Archives of General Psychiatry 11*, 1238–1245.

British Psychological Society (2000) *Guidance on the Assessment and Diagnosis of Intellectual Disabilities in Adulthood*. Leicester: British Psychological Society.

Brugha, T., Cooper, S.A., McManus, S. *et al.* (2012*) Estimating the Prevalence of Autism Spectrum Conditions in Adults: Extending the 2007 Adult Psychiatric Morbidity Survey*. London: NHS, The Health and Social Care Information Centre.

Butler-Sloss, E. (1988) *Report of the Enquiry into Child Abuse in Cleveland*. London: HMSO.

Carr, A. (2003) *The Handbook of Child and Adolescent Clinical Psychology: A Contextual Approach*. London: Brunner-Routledge Publications.

Cederlund, M., Hagberg, B. and Gillberg, C. (2010) 'Asperger syndrome in adolescent and young adult males: interview, self- and parent assessment of social, emotional, and cognitive problems.' *Research in Development Disabilities 31*, 287–298.

Champion, P. (2010) *CLDD Information Sheet*. Available at http://complexld.ssatrust.org.uk/uploads/attachment-info%20Aug.pdf, accessed on 13 June 2016.

Clarke, J. and van Amerom, G. (2008) 'Asperger's syndrome: differences between parents' understanding and those diagnosed.' *Social Work in Health Care 46*, 85–106.

Cleaver, H. and Nicholson, D. (2007) *Parental Learning Disability and Children's Needs: Family Experience and Effective Practice*. London: Jessica Kingsley Publishers.

Cleaver, H., Unell, I. and Aldgate, J. (1999) *Children's Needs: Parenting Capacity. The Impact of Parental Mental Illness, Problem Alcohol and Drug Use, and Domestic Violence on Children's Development*. London: The Stationery Office.

Cohen, B.Z. (1999) 'Measuring the willingness to seek help.' *Journal of Social Service Research 26*, 67–82.

Collins, N. and Read, S. (1990) 'Adult attachment, working models and relationship quality in dating couples.' *Journal of Personality and Social Psychology 58*, 644–663.

Coren, E., Thomae, M. and Hutchfield, J. (2011) 'Parenting training for intellectually disabled parents: a Cochrane systematic review.' *Research on Social Work Practice 21*, 4, 432–441.

Crittenden, P.M. and Landini, A. (2011) *Assessing Adult Attachment: A Dynamic-Maturational Approach to Discourse Analysis*. New York: W.W. Norton.

CSCI (Commission for Social Care Inspection) (2009) *Supporting Disabled Parents: A Family or a Fragmented Approach*. London: CSCI.

Davé, S., Petersen, I., Sherr, L. and Nazareth, I. (2010) 'Incidence of maternal and paternal depression in primary care: a cohort study using a primary care database.' *Archives of Pediatric and Adolescent Medicine 164*, 1038–1044.

DfE (Department for Education) (2015) *Working Together to Safeguard Children*. London: The Stationery Office.

DH (Department of Health) (2001) *Valuing People: A New Strategy for Learning Disability for the 21st Century*. London: The Stationery Office.

DH (2007) *Valuing People Now: From Progress to Transformation*. London: The Stationery Office.

DH (2009) *Valuing People Now: Summary Report March 2009 – September 2010*. London: The Stationery Office.

DH (2010a) *Making Written Information Easier to Understand for People with Learning Disabilities*. Available at www.gov.uk/government/uploads/system/uploads/attachment_data/file/215923/dh_121927.pdf, accessed on 13 June 2016.

DH (2010b) *Prioritising Need in the Context of Putting People First: A Whole System Approach to Eligibility for Social Care. Guidance on Eligibility Criteria for Adult Social Care*. London: Department of Health.

DH (2010c) *Valuing People Now: The Delivery Plan 2010–2011*. London: The Stationery Office.

DH and DfES (Department for Education and Skills) (2007) *Good Practice Guidance on Working with Parents with a Learning Disability*. London: The Stationery Office. Available at http://dera.ioe.ac.uk/6709/1/dh_075118.pdf, accessed on 13 June 2016.

DH, DfEE (Department for Education and Employment) and Home Office (2000) *Framework for the Assessment of Children in Need and Their Families*. London: The Stationery Office.

Disability Rights Commission (2006) *Easy Read: How to Use Easy Words and Pictures*. London: Disability Rights Commission.

Dodd, P. and McGinnity, M. (2003) 'Psychotherapy and learning disability.' *Irish Journal of Psychological Medicine 20*, 2, 38–40.

DWP (Department for Work and Pensions) and ODI (Office for Disability Issues) (2014) *Accessible Communication Formats*. Available at www.gov.uk/government/publications/inclusive-communication/accessible-communication-formats, accessed on 13 June 2016.

D'Zurilla, T.J and Nezu, A.M. (1999) *Problem-solving Therapy: A Social Competence Approach to Clinical Intervention*. New York: Springer.

Edgerton, R.B. (1967) *The Cloak of Competence: Stigma in the Lives of the Mentally Retarded*. Berkeley, CA: University of California Press.

Emerson, E. (2003) 'The prevalence of psychiatric disorders in children and adolescents with and without intellectual disabilities.' *Journal of Intellectual Disability Research 47*, 51–58.

Emerson, E. and Hatton, C. (2004) *Estimating the Current Need or Demand for Supports for People with Learning Disabilities in England*. Lancaster: Institute for Health Research, Lancaster University.

Emerson, E. and Hatton, C. (2007) 'The mental health of children and adolescents with intellectual disabilities in Britain.' *British Journal of Psychiatry 191*, 493–499.

Emerson, E., Malam, S., Davies, I. and Spencer, K. (2005) *Adults with Learning Difficulties in England 2003/4*. London: Office for National Statistics.

Fahlberg, V. (1991*) A Child's Journey through Placement*. Indianapolis, IN: Perspective Press.

Farmer, E., Sturgess, W. and O'Neill, T. (2008) *The Reunification of Looked After Children with Their Parents: Patterns, Interventions and Outcomes*. Report to the Department for Children, Schools and Families. Bristol: School for Policy Studies, University of Bristol.

Favrod, J., Linder, S., Pernier, S. and Chafloque, M.N. (2007) **'**Cognitive and behavioural therapy of voices for with patients intellectual disability: two case reports.' *Annals of General Psychiatry 6*, 22.

Feldman, M.A. (1994) 'Parenting education for parents with intellectual disability: a review of outcome studies.' *Research in Developmental Disabilities 15*, 299–307.

Feldman, M.A. (2002) 'Parents with Intellectual Disabilities and Their Children: Impediments and Supports.' In D. Griffiths and P. Federoff (eds) *Ethical Dilemmas: Sexuality and Developmental Disability*. Kingston, NY: NADD Press.

Feldman, M.A. (2010) 'Parenting Education Programmes.' In G. Llewellyn, R. Traustadottir, D. McConnell and H.B. Sigurjonsdottir (eds) *Parents with Intellectual Disabilities*. Chichester: J.Wiley & Sons.

Feninger-Schaal, R. (2010) 'Mother's resolution of the diagnosis of intellectual disability given to their children: associations with maternal sensitivity and children's security of attachment.' Unpublished dissertation, University of Haifa, Israel.

Fish, J., Manly, T., Kopelman, M. and Morris, R. (2015) 'Errorless learning of prospective memory tasks: an experimental investigation in people with memory disorders.' *Neuropsychological Rehabilitation 25*, 2, 159–188.

Flynn, M. and Russell, P. (2005) 'Adolescents and Younger Adults.' In G. Grant, P. Goward, M. Richardson and P. Ramcharam (eds) *Learning Disability: A Life Cycle Approach to Valuing People*. Maidenhead: Open University Press.

Focht-New, G., Clements, P.T., Barol, B., Faulkner, M.J. and Pekala, K. (2008) 'Persons with developmental disabilities exposed to interpersonal violence and crime: strategies and guidance for assessment.' *Perspectives in Psychiatric Care 44*, 1, 3–13.

Foundation for People with Learning Disabilities (2015) *Learning Disability: Postive Practice Guide*. London: Foundation for People with Learning Disabilities.

Frensch, P.A. and Funke, J. (eds) (1995) *Complex Problem Solving: The European Perspective*. Hillsdale, NJ: Lawrence Erlbaum Associates.

Gates, B. (2010) *The Valued People Project: Views of Parents and People with Learning Disabilities on Learning Disability Nursing and a Specialist Health Workforce for the Future*. Available at researchprofiles.herts.ac.uk/portal/files/131734/905176.pdf, accessed on 9 May 2016.

Gillberg, C., Rastam, M. and Wentz, E. (2001) 'The Asperger Syndrome (and highfunctioning autism) Diagnostic Interview (ASDI): a preliminary study of a newstructured clinical interview.' *Autism 5*, 57–66.

Glazemakers, I. and Deboutte, E. (2013) 'Modifying the "positive parenting programme" for parents with intellectual disabilties.' *Journal of Intellectual Disability Research 57*, 616–626.

Goldberg, B., Gitta, M.Z. and Puddephatt, A. (1995) 'Personality and trait disturbances in an adult mental retardation population: significance for psychiatric management.' *Journal of Intellectual Disability Research 39*, 284–294.

Golding, K. (2008) *Nurturing Attachments: Supporting Children Who Are Fostered or Adopted*. London: Jessica Kingsley Publishers.

Goodinge, S. (2000) *A Jigsaw of Services: Inspection of Services to Support Disabled Adults in Their Parenting Role*. London: DH.

Granqvist, P., Forslund, T., Springer, L., Fransson, M. and Lindberg, L. (2014) 'Mothers with intellectual disability, their experiences of maltreatment and their children's attachment representations: a small-group matched comparison study.' *Attachment & Human Development 16*, 417–436.

Gravestock, S. (2008) 'Eating disorders in adults with intellectual disability.' *Journal of Intellectual Disability Research 44*, 6, 625–637.

Gray, C. (2015) *The New Social Story Book*. Arlington, TX: Future Horizons Inc.

Green, G. and Vetere, A. (2002) 'Parenting, learning disabilities and inequality: can systematic thinking help?' *Clinical Psychology Forum 14*, 9–12.

Guinea, S.M. (2001) 'Parents with a learning disability and their views on support received: a preliminary study.' *Journal of Learning Disabilities 5*, 43–56.

Hazan, C. and Shaver, P. (1994) 'Attachment as an organizational framework for research on close relationship.' *Psychological Inquiry 5*, 1–22.

Heptinstall, E. and Taylor, E. (2002) 'Sex Differences and Their Significance.' In S. Sandberg (ed.) *Hyperactivity and Attention Disorders of Childhood* (2nd edn). Cambridge: Cambridge University Press.

Hoglund, B., Lindgren, P. and Larsson, M. (2012) 'Pregnancy and birth outcomes of women with intellectual disability in Sweden: a national register study.' *Acta Obstetricia Et Gynecologica Scandanavica 91*, 1381–1387.

Holburn, H., Perkins, T. and Vietze, P. (2001) 'The parent with mental retardation.' *International Review of Research in Mental Retardation 24*, 171–210.

Hollins, N. and Foley, A. (2013) 'The experiences of students with learning disabilities in a higher education virtual campus.' *Educational Research & Technology Development 61*, 4, 607–624.

Hove, O. (2004) 'Prevalence of eating disorders in adults with mental retardation living in the community.' *American Journal on Mental Retardation 109*, 501–506.

Howe, D. (2008) *The Emotionally Intelligent Social Worker*. Basingstoke: Palgrave Macmillan.

Hurlbutt, K. and Chalmers, L. (2002) 'Adults with autism speak out: perceptions of their life experiences.' *Focus on Autism and Other Developmental Disabilities 17*, 103–111.

Hurley, A.D. (2008) 'Depression in adults with intellectual disability: symptoms and challenging behaviour.' *Journal of Intellectual Disability Research 52*, 11, 905–916.

IASSID (International Association for the Scientific Study of Intellectual Disabilities) (2008) 'Parents labelled with intellectual disability: position of the IASSID SIRG on parents and parenting with intellectual disabilities.' *Journal of Applied Research in Intellectual Disabilities 21*, 296–307.

Jacques, R. (2003) 'Family issues.' *Psychiatry 2*, 9, September.

James, H. (2004) 'Promoting effective working with parents with learning disabilities.' *Child Abuse Review 13*, 1, 31–41.

Joop, D. and Keys, C. (2001) 'Diagnostic overshadowing reviewed and reconsidered.' *American Journal of Mental Retardation 6*, 416–433.

King's Fund Centre (1989) *Ties and Connections: An Ordinary Community Life for People with Learning Difficulties*. London: King's Fund Centre.

Kostro, K., Lerman, J.B. and Attia, E. (2014) 'The current status of suicide and self-injury in eating disorders: a narrative review.' *Journal of Eating Disorders 2*, 19.

Lamont, A. and Bromfield, L. (2009) 'Parental intellectual disability and child protection: key issues.' *NCPC Issues 31*. Available at https://aifs.gov.au/cfca/sites/default/files/publication-documents/issues31.pdf, accessed on 13 June 2016.

Larson, F.V., Alim, N. and Tsakanikos, E. (2011) 'Attachment style and mental health in adults with intellectual disability: self-reports and reports by carers.' *Advances in Mental Health and Intellectual Disabilities 5*, 3, 15 – 23.

LDO (Learning Disabilities Observatory), RCGP (Royal College of General Practitioners) and RCPsych (Royal College of Psychiatrists) (2012) *Improving the Health and Wellbeing of People with Learning Disabilities: An Evidence-Based Commissioning Guide for Clinical Commissioning Groups (CCGs)*. London: LDO, RCGP, RCPsych.

Lemay, R. (2012) 'The "cloak of competence": so who are we saying is stupid?' *Ethical Human Psychology and Psychiatry 14*, 2.

Levitas, A.S. and Gilson, S.F. (2001) 'Predictable crises in the lives of people with mental retardation.' *Mental Health Aspects of Developmental Disabilities 3*, 89–100.

Llewellyn, G. and McConnell, D. (2002) 'Mothers with learning difficulties and their support networks.' *Journal of Intellectual Disability Research 42*, 17–34.

Llewellyn, G., McConnell, D. and Bye, R. (1998) 'Perception of service needs by parents with intellectual disability, their significant others, and their service workers.' *Research in Developmental Disabilities 19*, 245–260.

Llewellyn, G., McConnell, D., Honey, A., Mayes, R. and Russo, D. (2003) 'Promoting health and home safety for children of parents with intellectual disability: a randomised controlled trial.' *Research in Developmental Disabilities 24*, 405–431.

Lord, C., Pickles, A., McLennan, J., Rutter, M. *et al.* (1997) 'Diagnosing autism: analyses of data from the Autism Diagnostic Interview.' *Journal of Autism and Developmental Disorders 27*, 501–517.

Lord, C., Risi, S., Lambrecht, L. *et al.* (2000) 'The Autism Diagnostic Observation Schedule-Generic: a standard measure of social and communication deficits associated with the spectrum of autism.' *Journal of Autism and Developmental Disorders 30*, 205–223.

McGaw, S. (1997) 'Practical Support for Parents with Learning Disabilities.' In J. O'Hara and A. Sperlinger (eds) *Adults with Learning Disabilities.* Chichester: John Wiley and Sons.

McGaw, S. (2007) *Parent Assessment Manual, 2nd Edn.* Truro: Pill Creek Publishing.

McGaw, S., Ball, K. and Clark, A. (2002) 'The effect of group intervention on the relationships of parents with intellectual disabilities.' *Journal of Applied Research in Intellectual Disabilities 15*, 354–366.

McGaw, S. and Newman, T. (2005) *What Works for Parents with Learning Disabilities?* Ilford: Barnados.

McGaw, S. and Sturmey, P. (1994) 'Assessing parents with learning disabilities: the parental skills model.' *Child Abuse Review 3*, 36–51.

McGaw, S., Scully, T. and Pritchard, C. (2010) 'Predicting the unpredictable? Identifying high-risk versus low-risk parents with intellectual disabilities.' *Child Abuse & Neglect 34*, 699–710.

McGaw, S., Shaw, T. and Beckley, K. (2007) 'Prevalence of psychopathology across a service population of parents with intellectual disabilities and their children.' *Journal of Policy and Practice in Intellectual Disabilities 4*, 1, 11–22.

McGaw, S., Beckley, K., Connolly, N. and Ball, K. (1998) *Parent Assessment Manual.* Truro: Trecare NHS Trust.

Main, M. and Solomon, J. (1986) 'Discovery of an Insecure Disorganized/Disorientated Attachment Pattern: Procedures, Findings and Implications for the Classification of Behaviour.' In M. Youngman and T.B. Brazelton (eds) *Affective Development in Infancy.* Norwood, NJ: Ablex.

Martorell, A. and Tsakanikos, E. (2008) 'Traumatic experiences and life events in people with intellectual disability.' *Current Opinion in Psychiatry 5*, 445–448.

Mason, J. and Scior, K. (2004) 'Diagnostic overshadowing amongst clinicians working with people with intellectual disabilities in the UK.' *Journal of Applied Research in Intellectual Disabilities 17*, 85–90.

Medlin, B. and Green, K.W. (2009) 'Enhancing performance through goal setting, engagement, and optimism.' *Industrial Management & Data Systems 109*, 7, 943–956.

Mencap (2007) *Providing the Right Support for Parents with a Learning Disability: Evaluating the Work of the North-East Parents' Support Service and the Walsall Parents' Advocacy Service.* London: Mencap.

Meppelder, M., Hodes, M., Kef, S. and Schuengel, C. (2014) 'Parents with intellectual disabilities seeking professional support: the role of working alliance, stress and informal support.' *Child Abuse & Neglect 38*, 9, 1478–1486.

Mevissen, L. and de Jongh, A. (2010) 'PTSD and its treatment in people with intellectual disabilities: a review of the literature.' *Clinical Psychology Review 30*, 308–316.

Milner, J. and O'Byrne, P. (2009) *Assessment in Social Work.* Basingstoke: Palgrave Macmillan.

Miltenberger, R. (2007) *Behaviour Modification: Principles and Procedures* (4th edn). Belmont, CA: Wadsworth.

Morgan, P. (2009) 'Using Mindfulness Meditation Therapy with People with Mild Intellectual Disabilities Who Have Generalised Anxiety Disorder.' Unpublished doctoral thesis, University of East Anglia.

Morgan, P. and Goff, A. (2004) *Learning Curves: The Assessment of Parents with a Learning Disability – A Manual for Practitioners.* Norwich: Norfolk Safeguarding Children Board.

Nader-Grosbois, N. (2007) *Régulation, Autorégulation, Dysrégulation.* Wavre: Mardaga.

Narang, D.S. and Contreras, J.M. (2005) 'The relationship of dissociation and affective family environment with the intergenerational cycle of child abuse.' *Child Abuse & Neglect 29*, 6, 683–699.

NICE (National Institute for Clinical Excellence) (2011) *Generalised Anxiety Disorder and Panic Disorder in Adults: Management.* Available at www.nice.org.uk/guidance/cg113/resources/generalised-anxiety-disorder-and-panic-disorder-in-adults-management-35109387756997, accessed on 13 June 2016.

NICE (2012) *Autism: Recognition, Referral, Diagnosis and Management of Adults on the Autism Spectrum* (Clinical Guidance 142). Available at http://guidance.nice.org.uk/CG142, accessed on 13 June 2016.

Norah Fry Research Centre (2009) *Supporting Parents with Learning Disabilities and Difficulties: Stories of Positive Practice.* Bristol: Norah Fry Research Centre.

O'Keeffe, N. and O'Hara, J. (2008) 'Mental health needs of parents with intellectual disabilities.' *Current Opinion in Psychiatry 21*, 5, 463–468.

Penketh, V., Hare, D.J., Flood, A. and Walker, S. (2014) 'Attachment in adults with intellectual disabilities: preliminary investigation of the psychometric properties of the Manchester attachment scale–third party observational measure.' *Journal of Applied Research in Intellectual Disabilities 27*, 5, 458–470.

Perkins T.S., Holburn S., Deaux, K., Flory, M.J. and Vietze, P.M. (2002) 'Children of mothers with intellectual disability: stigma, mother–child relationship and self-esteem.' *Journal of Applied Research in Intellectual Disabilities 15*, 297–313.

Poindexter, A.R. and Loschen, E. (2007) 'Eating Disorders.' In R.F. Fletcher, E. Loschen, C. Stavrakaki and F. Michael (eds) *Diagnostic Manual: Intellectual Disability.* New York: NADD Press.

Punshon, C., Skirrow, P. and Murphy, G. (2009) 'The "not guilty verdict": psychological reactions to a diagnosis of Asperger syndrome in adulthood.' *Autism 13*, 265–283.

RCN (Royal College of Nursing) (2010) *Mental Health Nursing of Adults with Learning Disabilities.* London: RCN.

Ritvo, R.A., Ritvo, E.R. and Guthrie, D. (2011) 'The Ritvo Autism Asperger Diagnostic Scale-Revised (RAADS-R): a scale to assist the diagnosis of autism spectrumdisorders in adults: an international validation study.' *Journal of Autism andDevelopmental Disorders 41*, 1076–1089.

Royal College of Psychiatrists (2001) *Diagnostic Criteria in Learning Disability (DC-LD).* London: Gaskell.

Schuengel, C., de Schipper, J.C., Sterkenburg, P.S. and Kef, S. (2013) 'Attachment, intellectual disabilities and mental health: research, assessment and intervention.' *Journal of Applied Research in Intellectual Disabilities 26*, 1, 34–46.

Schuetze, P. and Eiden, R.D. (2005) 'The relationship between sexual abuse during childhood and parenting outcomes: modeling direct and indirect pathways.' *Child Abuse & Neglect 29*, 6, 645–659.

Scottish Consortium for Learning Disabilities (2015) *Supported Parenting: Refreshed Scottish Good Practice Guidelines for Supporting Parents with a Learning Disability.* Available at www.scld.org.uk/wp-content/uploads/2015/06/Supported_Parenting_web.pdf, accessed on 25 July 2016.

Shogren, K., Bovaird, J., Palmer, S. and Wehmeyer, M. (2010) 'Locus of control orientations in students with intellectual disability, learning disabilities, and no disabilities: a latent growth curve analysis.' *Research & Practice for Persons with Severe Disabilities 35*, 3/4, 80.

Silverstone, P.H. and Salsali, M. (2003) 'Low self-esteem and psychiatric patients: part I – The relationship between low self-esteem and psychiatric diagnosis.' *Annals of General Psychiatry 2*, 1, 2.

Smale, G., Tuson, G. and Statham, D. (2000) *Social Work and Social Problems: Working towards Social Inclusion and Social Change.* London: Palgrave.

Smiley, E., Cooper, S.A., Finlayson, J., Jackson, A. *et al.* (2007) 'The incidence, and predictors of mental ill health in adults with intellectual disabilities: prospective study.' *British Journal of Psychiatry 191*, 313–319.

Starke, M. (2010) 'Encounters with professionals: views and experiences of mothers with intellectual disability.' *Journal of Intellectual Disabilities 14*, 1, 9–19.

Szidon, K. and Franzone, E. (2009) *Task Analysis.* Madison, WI: National Professional Development Center on Autism Spectrum Disorders, Waisman Center, University of Wisconsin.

Tantam, D. (2000) 'Psychological disorder in adolescents and adults with Asperger syndrome.' *Autism* 4, 47–62.

Tarleton, B. and Ward, L. (2007) 'Parenting with support: the views and experiences of parents with intellectual disabilities.' *Journal of Policy and Practice in Intellectual Disabilities* 4, 3, 194–202.

Tarleton, B., Ward, L. and Howarth, J. (2007) *Finding the Right Support? A Review of Issues and Positive Practice in Supporting Parents with Learning Difficulties and Their Children.* London: Baring Foundation.

Taylor, I. and Marrable, T. (2011) *Access to Social Care for Adults with Autistic Spectrum Conditions.* London: Social Care Institute for Excellence and University of Sussex.

Tomasulo, D.J. and Razza, N.J. (2007) 'Posttraumatic Stress Disorder.' In R. Fletcher, E. Loschen, C. Stavrakaki and M. First (eds) *Diagnostic Manual-Intellectual Disability (DM-ID): A Textbook of Diagnosis of Mental Disorders in Persons with Intellectual Disability.* Kingston, NY: NADD Press.

Traustadottir, R. and Sigurjonsdottir, H.B. (2010) 'Parenting and Resistance: Strategies in Dealing with Services and Professionals.' In G. Llewellyn, R. Traustadottir, D. McConnell and H.B. Sigurjonsdottir (eds) *Parents with Intellectual Disabilities.* Chichester: J. Wiley and Sons.

Trotter, K. (1997) 'Nutrition and eating disorders.' *Nursing Times 93*, 46, 1–6.

Turney, D., Platt, D., Selwyn, J. and Farmer, E. (2012) *Improving Child and Family Assessments: Turning Research into Practice.* London: Jessica Kingsley Publishers.

Tymchuk, A.J. (1992b) 'Project parenting: child interactional training with mothers who are mentally handicapped.' *Mental Handicap Research 5*, 4–32.

van der Kolk, B.A. (1996) 'The Complexity of Adaptation to Trauma: Self-regulation, Stimulus Discrimination and Characterological Development.' In B.A. van der Kolk, A.C. McFarlane and L. Weisaeth (eds) *Traumatic Stress: The Effects of Overwhelming Experience on Mind, Body and Society.* New York: Guilford Press.

Wade, J., Biehal, N., Farrelly, N. and Sinclair, I. (2010) *Outcomes for Children Looked After for Reasons of Abuse or Neglect: The Consequences of Staying in Care or Returning Home.* DFE-RBX-10-06. London: Department for Education.

Wade, C., Llewellyn, G. and Matthews, J. (2008) 'Review of parent training interventions for parents with intellectual disabilities.' *Journal of Applied Research in Intellectual Disabilities 21*, 351–366.

Wagner, K.D. (2011) Effects of early parental depression.' *Psychiatric Times.* Available at www.psychiatrictimes.com/major-depressive-disorder/effects-early-parental-depression, accessed on 13 June 2016.

Ward, H., Brown, R., Westlake, D. and Munro, E. (2010) *Infants Suffering, or Likely to Suffer, Significant Harm: A Prospective Longitudinal Study.* Research Brief DFE-RB053. London: Department for Education.

Ward, L. and Tarleton, B. (2007) 'Sinking or swimming? Supporting parents with learning disabilities and their children.' *Learning Disability Review 12*, 2, 22–32.

WHO (World Health Organization) (1996) *International Statistical Classification of Diseases and Related Health Problems*, 10th Revision (ICD-10). Geneva: WHO.

Willis, T.J., LaVigna, G.W. and Donnellan, A.M. (1993) *Behavior Assessment Guide.* Los Angeles, CA: Institute for Applied Behavior Analysis.

Wilson, P., Rush, R., Hussey, S., Puckering, C. *et al.* (2012) 'How evidence-based is an "evidence-based parenting program"? A PRISMA systematic review and meta-analysis of Triple P.' *BMC Medicine 10*, 230, 1–16.

Wilson, S., McKenzie, K., Quayle, E. and Murray, G. (2013) 'A systematic review of interventions to promote social support and parenting skills in parents with an intellectual disability.' *Child: Care, Health and Development 40*, 1, 7–19.

Wing, L. (2003) *Diagnostic Interview for Social and Communication Disorders* (11th edn). London: National Autistic Society.

Wood, J. (2010) *Interpersonal Communication: Everyday Encounters.* Boston, MA: Wadsworth-Cengage Learning.

Young, S. (2005) 'Coping strategies used by adults with ADHD.' *Personality and Individual Differences 38*, 4, 809–816.

Young, S. and Strouthos, M. (1998) *First Steps to Parenthood.* Brighton: Pavilion.

Subject Index

Author Index